PARTY
FOOD
for *girls*

Mindy Cone

FRONT TABLE BOOKS

An Imprint of Cedar Fort, Inc.
Springville, Utah

ISBN 13: 978-1-4621-1338-5

Published by Front Table Books, an imprint of Cedar Fort, Inc.
2373 W. 700 S., Springville, UT 84663
Distributed by Cedar Fort, Inc., www.cedarfort.com

Library of Congress Cataloging-in-Publication Data

Cone, Mindy, author.
Party food for girls : lovely and luscious recipes, party ideas, and styling tips for your next event / Mindy Cone.
    pages cm
Includes index.
ISBN 978-1-4621-1338-5
1. Parties. 2. Entertaining. 3. Appetizers. I. Title.
TX731.C64 2014
642'.4--dc23
                        2013040864

Cover and page design by Erica Dixon
Cover design © 2014 by Lyle Mortimer
Edited by Casey J. Winters

Printed in China

10 9 8 7 6 5 4 3 2 1

Dedicated to my mother, my sisters & my daughter

HILARY, AMANDA, TAYLOR, AND AUBREY

contents

Acknowledgments

I would not be able to do any of this without my amazing family behind me! Thank you, Randall, for your continued support of all my creative endeavors. Thank you to my children, Aubrey and Patton, for being the best taste testers around! You are always so willing to lend your services for each new recipe . . . particularly the desserts! To my mother—the ultimate hostess—thank you for inspiring me to be creative in the kitchen and entertain with style. To my family—Dad, Mandy, Ryan, and Taylor—your love and support has kept me going. Thank you for encouraging me to reach for my dreams and truly believing that I would achieve them. I am honored to have such wonderful friends and extended family who have cheered me on during this journey. Thank you for always being there for me!

I have been blessed to meet and connect with so many talented and creative people through *Creative Juice*, many of whom have become great friends. I could never have imagined when I began this journey the magnitude of your support, generosity, and outpouring of love! A special thank-you to all of the vendors who collaborated and donated party items to be included in the styling of this book. I am honored to be a part of such an incredible network of creative genius to rely on.

Of course I want to say thank you to all of the supportive and amazing fans of *Creative Juice*! Whether you follow along through Facebook, Twitter, or Instagram, or subscribe to the blog, *you* are the reason I am able to achieve this dream. Your comments make my day. Your emails bring me huge smiles. Your encouraging words and thoughtful sentiments have connected us on so many occasions—and I am so thankful for you!

I would be just a girl with a dream to write a book had it not been for the incredible team from Cedar Fort Publishing. Thank you for believing in me, for understanding my vision, and for bringing something from my dreams into reality. Thank you, Joanna Barker, Erica Dixon, Casey Winters, and the entire Cedar Fort team for all you have done!

Be the *Ultimate* Hostess

This book is the perfect marriage of everything I love: fun parties, great food, delicious desserts, and mouthwatering snacks—all with a girly twist!

I definitely inherited my love for hosting events from the ultimate hostess: my mother! Growing up, our home was the center of dinner parties, game nights, graduation celebrations, and more. Every event was elegant, beautiful, and, of course, delicious. I learned to cook from my mother—using my intuition, taste testing along the way, and experimenting. Not only did I inherit my mother's hostess gene, but I also cultivated an excitement for developing recipes and trying new things.

While I always loved hosting events for my friends, when I had children this love for hosting only intensified! I was catapulted into the world of party styling, dessert tables, whimsical party food, crafty party ideas, budget tips, and more—all of which I share on my blog, *Creative Juice*. While some people dread party planning, I revel in it! I love pouring myself into all the creative details: adorable food presentation, unique crafted backdrops, out-of-the-box party favors, and exciting activities.

Throughout my experiences, I have hosted many events for girls and women of all ages—birthday parties, baby showers, bridal showers, bachelorette parties, sip-n-sees, gender-reveal parties, graduation parties, and a lot of girls' nights! This book is a collection of my favorite recipes I serve at these events. Each recipe will have tips for preparing the food in advance and how to style it so that everyone will ooh and ahh over your presentation. Now *you* will be the ultimate hostess!

Girly
STYLING TIPS

Each recipe in this book will have specific ideas for styling, but here are some general ideas for making your party food girly and fun.

Use Bright Colors

It doesn't have to be pink and purple to be girly! Teal, yellow, red, orange, or even black and white can be striking.

Use Fun Patterns

Flower prints are girly, but they are not the only way to go. Use polka dots, damask, stripes, chevron, or anything fun.

Use Individual Servings

This adds a personalized touch to every party and makes the guest feel special and important—what every girl wants!

Miniaturize It

Let's face it—miniature food is adorable and girly.

Serve It on a Stick

This is a dainty and exciting way to eat. Plus, it gives you an opportunity to add more decorative elements to the dish!

Add Decorative, Crafty Touches

Use ribbon, washi tape, fabric strips, or twine to add detail and decorative touches for a fancy feeling.

Use Adorable Party Products and Containers

Use striped straws, favor bags, cupcake liners, wax party cups, paper ice cream cups, bamboo utensils, patterned paper fry boxes, patterned baking trays, and cute cups and plates. You can find many amazing party resources out there.

Use Fruit as a Bowl

This is a fun, fresh, and girly way to serve a dish.

Buy Digital Printables

This is a great way to bring a custom girly theme to life. Online shop owners have created printable party packages tailored to your event. You can print personalized party items such as cupcake toppers and favor tags to embellish your recipes and décor.

Bring Out the Nice Platters and Servingware

Use real plates, cake stands, and utensils. This will make your guests feel like princesses!

Cut Food in a Unique Way

Use cookie cutters to cut fruit and sandwiches, use a melon baller, or make triangular cuts. All of these things make something ordinary into something unique!

Use Classic Girly Shapes and Icons

Use, for example, stars, hearts, swirls, flowers, butterflies, bows, pearls, high heels, crowns, and purses.

Use Flavor Profiles

I have found that girls and women enjoy flavor profiles on either end of the spectrum—bright, fruity, light, and fresh or decadent and rich.

Use Fresh Flowers and Fresh Fruit

to decorate and garnish your recipes!

Decorate with candy,

add sprinkles, and use edible shimmer!

It's the little things at an event that really make it special—but the party doesn't have to be complicated! These simple ideas can transform your party. You can find so many amazing party supplies out there—many of which I will reference throughout this book. I've included a complete list of resources at the end of this book so you can find the party supplies you are looking for!

Party Planning Tips & Timeline

Each recipe in this book will have tips for party preparation. This will tell you how far in advance you can make, bake, frost, reheat, refrigerate, or freeze the recipe. There is a lot more to a party than just food—although for me that is the most important part! Here is an outline for basic party planning that will help you along the way.

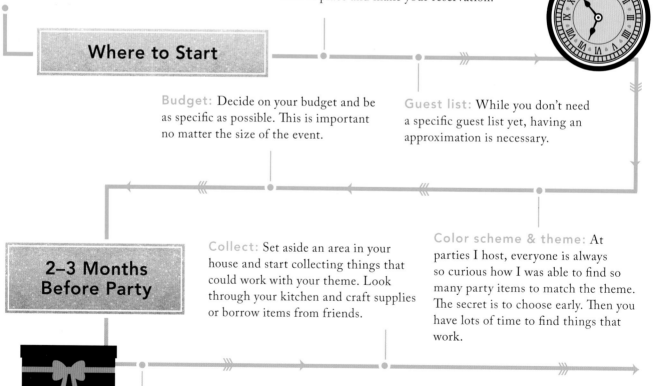

Making these decisions early will make party planning much less stressful. I typically choose these things about three months in advance for a medium-size party.

Location and date: If you are hosting at your home, you have some wiggle room with the date and can make this decision as it gets closer. If you are renting the space, be sure to have a specific date in place and make your reservation.

Where to Start

Budget: Decide on your budget and be as specific as possible. This is important no matter the size of the event.

Guest list: While you don't need a specific guest list yet, having an approximation is necessary.

2–3 Months Before Party

Collect: Set aside an area in your house and start collecting things that could work with your theme. Look through your kitchen and craft supplies or borrow items from friends.

Color scheme & theme: At parties I host, everyone is always so curious how I was able to find so many party items to match the theme. The secret is to choose early. Then you have lots of time to find things that work.

Order online products: The amazing online party shops listed in the resources section at the end of this book will have adorable items and details to match any theme. Often these details are what make the party so perfect.

Custom paper printables: These take time to create, so if you have not found exactly what you want in an online shop, be sure to get in touch with a designer early to start the custom work. (See the resources list for designers.)

Keep an eye out while shopping: You never know where you will find something that fits your theme!

Reserve rental equipment & professionals: Order the cake, hire a photographer, and reserve tables, chairs, and linens, and so on.

Supplies: Begin gathering nonperishable supplies from local stores (see resources list): plates, napkins, cake stands, and utensils.

1 Month Before

Set your guest list and send invitations: I like the traditional route of mailing or hand-delivering the invite—especially if it is a children's party. My daughter gets so excited when she receives mail, and she hangs the invitation in her room. However, email invites are convenient and popular, with lots of adorable premade styles to choose from. Whichever route you choose, be sure to triple-check your spelling and information—I know this from personal experience! I may or may not have sent everyone to an incorrect location for an event once . . .

Plan your menu: Choose recipes that fit your theme based on color, style, and flavors.

Choose your activities: Gather supplies and make a plan. I generally try to have 2–3 activities at each party.

Follow up with all hired items and confirm reservations.

1 Week Before

Printable party décor: If you are using these, now is the time to print, cut, and assemble.

Assemble nonperishable goodie bags and party favors.

Buy nonperishable recipe ingredients and supplies.

If hosting at your house, clean and stock up on bathroom and kitchen consumables.

3 Days Before

Charge batteries on cameras and video equipment.

Food preparation: Some of the recipes in this book can be prepared this early. Be sure to check the "party prep" portion of the recipe to see how early you can start cooking.

Buy perishable ingredients.

Set up everything you can—activities, dessert and food tables with linens, printables, decorations, and favors.

Food preparation: Check your recipes and see what you can check off your list!

Prepare recipes that will keep in the refrigerator overnight.

Refrigerate drinks.

1 Day Before

Charge your phone: You will want to share this day on social media, so be sure you can snap a few photos on your phone.

If you are taking pictures yourself, have everything set up with enough time before your guests arrive.

Relax and Enjoy!

Be a guest at your own party!

Put up last-minute decorations.

Day of Party

Set out food on tables.

Buy last-minute items—balloons, ice for coolers, and so on.

Prepare last-minute food and reheat recipes.

Savory Appetizers & Snacks

It can't always be sweet! Serve these savory recipes to your guests as appetizers, hors d'oeuvres, or snacks—whether you are hosting a casual get-together or a formal event.

Cucumber Rounds with Lemon Ricotta Cheese & Roasted Tomatoes

Makes 15–20 cucumber bites

Ingredients

1	cup heavy cream
3	cups whole milk
1	cup buttermilk
1	lemon, zest and juice
10–12	cherry tomatoes
3	Tbsp. olive oil
1	tsp. salt
3	cucumbers

Party prep: These can be made and assembled the day before the party. Line an airtight container with a damp paper towel and place prepared cucumber bites on top. Store in the refrigerator and serve cold.

Styling ideas: Dress these up with a fun little red flag! I took decorative washi tape, folded it over a wooden toothpick, and cut a little triangle out of the end. It is very simple but is a great way to add a punch of color to your food. Prepare the toothpicks ahead of time and place in the cucumbers before serving.

Directions:

- Heat heavy cream, milk, buttermilk, and lemon zest and juice in a nonreactive pan over medium heat until it begins to simmer.

- While heating, place cheesecloth (double layered) into a strainer over the top of a bowl or in the sink.

- Continue to simmer and occasionally stir until the mixture begins to separate into curds.

- Pour mixture carefully into the cheesecloth, allowing the liquid to drain through.

- Allow to rest in the strainer for 15–20 minutes and then bring the ends of the cheesecloth up and tie at the top. Allow to rest for another 15 minutes.

- Remove lemon ricotta cheese from the cheesecloth and place in an airtight container in the refrigerator for up to 3 days if you are not using it immediately.

- Preheat oven to 400 degrees.

- Cut cherry tomatoes in half lengthwise and place on a sheet pan. Drizzle with olive oil and sprinkle with salt.

- Roast tomatoes at 400 degrees for 5–7 minutes.

- Remove tomatoes and allow to cool.

- Peel cucumbers, leaving strips of the skin every ¼ inch.

- Remove the ends of the cucumber and cut 1-inch rounds.

- Using a melon baller, scoop out half the thickness of the seeds in each round.

- Place a small dollop of lemon ricotta cheese on the cucumber and top with a roasted tomato.

Savory Appetizers & Snacks

Mushroom & Onion Phyllo Cups

Makes 20–25 pastry bites

Ingredients

½ onion, finely chopped

3 Tbsp. butter, divided

4 cups finely chopped mushrooms

1 clove garlic, minced

1 tsp. salt

1 tsp. pepper

2 Tbsp. flour

2 Tbsp. Worcestershire sauce

4 oz. cream cheese

20–25 prepared phyllo cups

chives (optional)

Party prep: Filling can be made up to 2 days in advance and stored in an airtight container in the refrigerator. Prepare phyllo cups as directed in recipe but cook at 325 degrees for 10 minutes or until heated through. Serve immediately.

Styling ideas: For these, I loved the ruffled edge of the phyllo cups, so all I added was some chopped chives as a garnish and a pop of color. They are bite-size, so serving them on a tiered platter would be adorable!

Directions:

• Sauté onions in 2 tablespoons of butter until caramelized.

• Add mushrooms, garlic, and 1 tablespoon of butter and continue to sauté until cooked through.

• Add salt, pepper, flour, and Worcestershire sauce and stir over low heat.

• Place cream cheese into the sauté pan, stir until fully incorporated, and then remove from the heat.

• Preheat oven to 375 degrees.

• Line a sheet pan with prepared phyllo cups and fill each with a tablespoon of mushroom filling.

• Cook at 375 degrees for 4–5 minutes or until phyllo is crispy.

• Garnish with chopped chives, if desired, and serve immediately.

Savory Appetizers & Snacks

Baked Herbed Pita Chips

Makes 6–8 servings

Ingredients

4   pita pockets

¼   cup olive oil

dry herbs and spices:
rosemary, garlic powder,
parsley, oregano, onion
powder, salt, pepper

Party prep: These can be made 2–3 days in advance. Store in an airtight container.

Styling ideas: Serve with Sun-Dried Tomato Hummus (p. 14) family style or in small individual cups with 3–4 pita chips.

Directions:

- Preheat oven to 400 degrees.

- Cut each pita pocket into 8 triangles and arrange in a single layer on a sheet pan. Combine olive oil and dry herbs and spices in a small dish. With a food brush, apply the oil and herb mixture to the pita triangles.

- Cook for 7–10 minutes or until pita chips are crispy.

Sun-Dried Tomato Hummus

Makes 6–8 servings

Ingredients

1	(16-oz.) can chickpeas
1½	Tbsp. tahini
1	lemon, zest and juice
2	cloves garlic
1	Tbsp. sesame oil
½	cup sun-dried tomatoes (in oil)
2	Tbsp. oil from sun-dried tomatoes
½	tsp. salt

Party prep: This can be made up to 3 days in advance if kept refrigerated. Bring to room temperature before serving.

Styling ideas: Serve family style or in small individual cups with 3–4 Baked Herbed Pita Chips (p. 12). Garnish with strips of sun-dried tomatoes.

Directions:

• Place all ingredients in blender or food processor and blend until smooth.

Basic Dip Base

Makes about 2½ cups

Ingredients

4   oz. cream cheese, room temperature

1   cup sour cream

½   cup mayonnaise

Party prep: This can be divided and flavored immediately for storage or serving, or stored plain until the day of the party. By using this basic dip recipe, you can impress your guests with myriad flavor options and cut down on your prep time.

Directions:

• Blend ingredients together until fully incorporated.

Chipotle Dipping Sauce

Makes 6–8 servings

Ingredients

1   recipe Basic Dip Base
    (p. 15)

4   Tbsp. chipotle adobo
    sauce

1   tsp. garlic powder

1   tsp. onion powder

    salt and pepper
    to taste

Party prep: Admittedly I am a spice wimp, so this is on the mild to medium side. Add additional heat with more chipotle adobo sauce. Dip will strengthen in heat as it sits. This can be prepared and served immediately or stored in the refrigerator until the day of the party.

Styling ideas: Serve this with Rustic Roasted Potato Wedges (p. 19).

Directions:

•   Combine all ingredients into a small bowl.

17

Fresh Dill Dip

Makes about 2½ cups

Ingredients

1 recipe Basic Dip Base
(p. 15)

1 tsp. onion powder

½ cup finely chopped
fresh dill

salt and pepper
to taste

Party prep: This can be prepared and served immediately or stored in the refrigerator until the day of the party.

Styling ideas: Serve this at the bottom of individual cups such as the Fresh Veggie Cups (p. 21).

Directions:

• Combine all ingredients in a small bowl.

Savory Appetizers & Snacks

Cilantro Dip

Makes 6–8 servings

Ingredients

1   recipe Basic Dip Base
     (p. 15)

1   garlic clove

2   Tbsp. white vinegar

2   Tbsp. lime juice

1   large bunch of cilantro

1   tsp. Tabasco sauce

1   pkg. dry ranch dressing
     mix

Party prep: This is definitely a girls-only party recipe! It is one of my favorites—but you may want to serve breath mints afterward! It is worth it, though. This can be prepared and served immediately or stored in the refrigerator until the day of the party. Flavor will intensify when stored.

Styling ideas: Serve this at the bottom of individual cups such as the Tomato Mini Skewers (p. 22).

Directions:

• Place all ingredients into a blender or food processor.

• Blend until you reach a smooth consistency.

Rustic Roasted Potato Wedges

Makes about 10 servings

Ingredients

6–8   large baking potatoes

⅓   cup olive oil

2   tsp. seasoned salt

Party prep: These can be made ahead of time (no more than 2 days recommended) and reheated in the oven prior to serving.

Styling ideas: I love to serve these with Chipotle Dipping Sauce (p. 16) and serve them in cute hot dog trays. That way the girls can grab an individual serving and mingle as they eat!

Directions:

- Preheat oven to 400 degrees.

- Cut potatoes in half lengthwise. Cut each potato half into 4 wedges lengthwise.

- Line a baking sheet with parchment paper or a silpat and lay the wedges in a single layer.

- Use a food brush to spread olive oil on each wedge.

- Sprinkle each wedge with seasoned salt.

- Bake for 40–50 minutes or until potatoes are browned and crisp.

Savory Appetizers & Snacks

Fresh Veggie Cups

Makes 10–12 servings

Ingredients

5	carrot sticks
1	red pepper
3	stalks of celery
1	cucumber
1	recipe Fresh Dill Dip (p. 17)
	sprigs of fresh dill

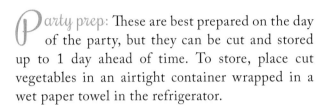

Party prep: These are best prepared on the day of the party, but they can be cut and stored up to 1 day ahead of time. To store, place cut vegetables in an airtight container wrapped in a wet paper towel in the refrigerator.

Styling ideas: I like to serve these individually because, while a vegetable tray is a favorite at any party, it's boring! With just a little extra time, you can dress up a classic option for your guests. Try to choose vegetables within your color scheme for the party!

Directions:

- Cut vegetables lengthwise to accommodate for the size of your serving cups.

- Spoon dill dip into the bottom of your serving cups.

- Arrange vegetables into the cups and garnish with sprigs of fresh dill.

Savory Appetizers & Snacks

Tomato Mini Skewers with Cilantro Dip

Makes 10–15 servings

Ingredients

2   pints cherry tomatoes

1   recipe Cilantro Dip
    (p. 18)

Party prep: The dip can be prepared and served immediately or stored in the refrigerator until the day of the party. Flavor will intensify when stored. I recommend waiting until the day of the party to skewer the tomatoes.

Styling ideas: Place a small amount of the cilantro dip into the base of a small serving cup and place the tomato skewer inside for miniature individual servings.

Directions:

• Wash and dry cherry tomatoes.

• Carefully slide 4–5 cherry tomatoes each on large toothpicks.

• Serve with Cilantro Dip.

Caprese Skewers with Balsamic Dressing

Makes 10–15 servings

Ingredients

1   pint cherry tomatoes

1   bunch fresh basil

16   oz. fresh mozzarella cheese

1   cup balsamic dressing

Party prep: Mozzarella can be cubed up to 2 days in advance and stored in an airtight container in the refrigerator. I recommend waiting until the day of the party to assemble the skewers.

Styling ideas: Place a small amount of the balsamic dressing into the base of small serving cups and place the Caprese Skewers inside for miniature individual servings.

Directions:

- Wash and dry cherry tomatoes and basil leaves.

- Cut mozzarella into ½-inch cubes.

- Carefully slide a cherry tomato on a large toothpick. Follow with a folded basil leaf and a cube of mozzarella. Repeat until the toothpick is full. Repeat for all toothpicks.

- Serve with balsamic dressing.

Savory Appetizers & Snacks

Baked Sweet Potato Skins

Makes 12–15 servings

Ingredients

3–4 sweet potatoes

2 Tbsp. olive oil

1½ cups sour cream

½ cup chopped chives

½ cup crumbled bacon

Party prep: Sweet potato skins can be prepared up to 2 days in advance. Stop after cutting the skins into bite-size pieces. In an airtight container, separate each layer with wax paper and store in the refrigerator. When ready to serve, heat in the oven at 400 degrees for 15–20 minutes, or until skin is crisp, and add toppings before serving.

Styling ideas: Since these are assembled right before serving and have a rustic feel to them, I generally keep the styling minimal and serve them on a platter.

Directions:

- Preheat oven to 400 degrees.

- Clean sweet potatoes and pierce 6–8 holes into each.

- Brush each sweet potato with olive oil.

- Cook sweet potatoes on a baking sheet for 40–50 minutes or until cooked through.

- Remove and allow to cool enough to handle.

- Slice each potato in half lengthwise.

- Scoop out the center, leaving the skin and a thin layer of potato. Cut in half again for more bite-size pieces.

- If serving immediately, place back in the oven for 10–15 minutes or until the skins are crisp.

- Remove sweet potato skins and top with sour cream, chives, and crumbled bacon.

Fresh Texas Salsa

Makes about 6 cups

Ingredients

1	(16-oz.) can corn
1	(16-oz.) can black beans
1	(16-oz.) can black-eyed peas
2	large tomatoes
½	medium red onion
1	pepper (yellow, orange, green, or red)
1	bunch cilantro
2	garlic cloves, grated
¼	cup oil
¼	cup vinegar
2	limes, zest and juice
1	Tbsp. sugar
1	tsp. Tabasco sauce
1	tsp. cumin
	salt and pepper to taste
3	avocados, diced

Party prep: If preparing more than 4 hours in advance, make the recipe as directed excluding the avocado. Store in the refrigerator for up to 24 hours. Add the avocado right before serving.

Styling ideas: These would be fun to serve individually, but sometimes the girls like to sit around the platter and chat while they snack! This would be great for any rustic themed party or even a summer get-together!

Directions:

• Drain and rinse corn, black beans, and black-eyed peas and place in a large bowl.

• Dice tomatoes, red onion, and pepper. Roughly chop cilantro leaves. Add these ingredients to the bowl.

• In a small bowl, whisk together grated garlic cloves, oil, vinegar, the zest and juice of both limes, sugar, Tabasco sauce, and cumin.

• Pour dressing over the large bowl and stir to combine.

• Add salt and pepper to taste.

• Cover and refrigerate for 2 hours.

• Before serving, add diced avocados and stir to combine.

Savory Appetizers & Snacks

Sweet Appetizers & Snacks

Every girl loves a sweet snack! From fruit to chocolate, these recipes will have your guests happy and snacking at your party. They are great for any occasion.

Strawberries & Cream Fruit Dip

Makes about 3 cups

Ingredients

1   (8-oz.) pkg. strawberry
     cream cheese, room
     temperature

1   cup powdered sugar

1   (6-oz.) container
     strawberry yogurt

1   (7-oz.) container
     spreadable marshmallow

Party prep: This can be made up to 3 days in advance and kept in the refrigerator.

Styling ideas: I love this recipe for girly parties because it's pink! It goes perfectly with any dessert or food table with a pink color scheme.

Directions:

• Cream together strawberry cream cheese, powdered sugar, and yogurt.

• Mix in spreadable marshmallow to desired consistency.

Rainbow Fruit Cups

Makes 12–15 servings

Ingredients

4   cups sliced strawberries

4   cups balled cantaloupe

4   cups cut pineapple

4   cups green grapes or cut kiwifruit

4   cups blueberries

4   cups red grapes

Party prep: I recommend preparing the fruit no more than 6 hours before the party. Store in the refrigerator until serving.

Styling ideas: I love using adorable colorful baking cups to serve the fruit! You can place each color of fruit in a coordinating cup. I have also served them on skewers so that each person receives a rainbow fruit skewer!

Directions:

• Place bite-size fruit in separate cups.

Sweet Appetizers & Snacks

Melon Cups

Makes 8–10 servings

Ingredients

8   cups balled or cubed honeydew melon

8   cups balled or cubed cantaloupe

Party prep: I recommend preparing the fruit no more than 6 hours before the party. Store in the refrigerator until serving.

Styling ideas: The colors in this dish are so fun—bright green and orange! I served these in green striped cups, but orange cups would be adorable too.

Directions:

• Place balled or cubed honeydew melon and cantaloupe in small cups, mixing the colors.

Green Fruit Skewers

Makes about 8 servings

Ingredients

1 honeydew melon

2 apples

2 pears

4 kiwifruits

2 cups green grapes

Party prep: I recommend preparing the fruit no more than 6 hours before the party. Add the melons to the skewer right before displaying. Spritz fruit skewers with a little bit of lemon juice to avoid oxidation.

Styling ideas: Add a little ribbon or washi tape to the top of the skewer for some extra flair!

Directions:

- Cut honeydew melon into large rectangles—these will be the bases of your skewers.

- Dice apple and pear into bite-size pieces (do not remove skin).

- Remove kiwifruit skin and slice horizontally into thick circles.

- To assemble, slide the apples, pears, grapes, and kiwifruit pieces onto the bottom half of the skewer.

- Use the rectangular melon as the base of the skewer so that it will stand upright.

- Display on a flat serving dish.

Sweet Appetizers & Snacks

Fruity Candied Popcorn

Makes about 8 servings

Ingredients

3   Tbsp. butter

2   Tbsp. corn syrup

3   Tbsp. sugar

3   Tbsp. powdered drink mix*

9   cups popped popcorn

*I used orange in this recipe, but
you can use any flavored drink mix
as long as it is not sugar-free.*

Party prep: This can be made up to 3 days ahead of time and stored in a cool, dry container.

Styling ideas: This recipe can be adapted to tons of different colors and flavor profiles to match any party theme! I love mixing different flavors of popcorn into a clear bag as a colorful favor for guests.

Directions:

• Preheat oven to 275 degrees and line a sheet pan with parchment paper.

• Melt butter in a small saucepan and add corn syrup, sugar, and drink mix.

• Increase heat and bring to a simmer.

• Continue to stir on low heat for about 5 minutes.

• Pour mixture over popcorn in a large bowl and immediately toss to coat. Use caution—mixture is very hot.

• Spread coated popcorn onto your sheet pan and cook for 7 minutes.

• Remove from oven and allow to cool enough to handle. Break popcorn apart into pieces and serve.

Cake Batter Popcorn

Makes about 8 servings

Ingredients

1½   cups white chocolate chips

⅓   cup vegetable oil

1¾   cup white cake mix

9   cups popped popcorn

¾   cup multicolored jimmy sprinkles, divided

 Party prep: This can be made up to 1 day ahead of time and stored in a cool, dry container.

 Styling ideas: This recipe can be adapted to different flavor profiles to match any party theme—simply use different cake mixes!

Directions:

- Melt chocolate chips and stir in vegetable oil and cake mix.

- Drizzle over popcorn in a large bowl and toss to coat.

- Sprinkle with ½ cup jimmy sprinkles and toss to coat.

- Spread coated popcorn on parchment paper.

- Sprinkle remaining jimmy sprinkles over the top.

- Leave at room temperature or chill in the fridge for chocolate to harden.

Sweet Appetizers & Snacks

Chocolate Snack Mix

Makes about 6 servings

Ingredients

½ cup melted chocolate, divided

1 tsp. vegetable oil

2 cups corn cereal (Chex brand)

½ cup powdered sugar

1 cup honey roasted peanuts

¼ cup Crunch chocolate bits

1 cup mini marshmallows

¼ cup brown mini M&M's

¼ cup melted white chocolate

¼ cup chocolate jimmy sprinkles

 Party prep: This can be made up to 1 day ahead of time and stored in an airtight container.

 Styling ideas: This is one of my favorite snacks. The mix is great for late-night sleepovers or chick flick movie nights. Or it makes a great favor at any girly party, packaged in a glassine favor bag—what girl doesn't love chocolate?

Directions:

- Combine ¼ cup melted chocolate and oil. Pour over cereal and toss to coat.

- Place chocolate-covered cereal in a large plastic bag with powdered sugar and shake to coat.

- Spread on wax paper and allow to cool.

- In a large bowl, combine peanuts, Crunch bits, marshmallows, mini M&M's, and cooled chocolate cereal.

- Spread mixture onto wax paper and drizzle with remaining ¼ cup melted chocolate and melted white chocolate.

- Sprinkle with chocolate jimmies and allow to cool.

Pink Cherry Snack Mix

Makes about 6 servings

Ingredients

1   cup melted white chocolate

2   tsp. vegetable oil

4   cups corn cereal (Chex brand)

¾   cup powdered sugar

1   packet cherry powdered Kool-Aid mix

1   cup mini marshmallows

1   cup pink mini marshmallows

1   cup dark chocolate raspberry M&M's*

 * I use the two lighter pink colors in the mix

Party prep: This can be made up to 1 day ahead of time and stored in an airtight container.

Styling ideas: I like to serve this mix in cute popcorn bags. It's great for late-night sleepovers or chick flick movie nights. Or package them in a glassine bag for a great favor at any girly party.

Directions:

• Combine melted white chocolate and oil. Pour over cereal and toss to coat.

• Place chocolate-covered cereal in a large plastic bag with powdered sugar and cherry drink mix. Shake to coat.

• Spread on wax paper and allow to cool.

• Once cooled, combine with marshmallows and M&M's.

Sweet Appetizers & Snacks

Breakfast & Brunch

These recipes and styling ideas are so much fun to wake up to!
Whether you have a party early in the day or are serving slumber
party guests, these ideas are worth waking up for!

Butterscotch Mini Monkey Bread

Makes about 16 muffins

Ingredients

2	(16-oz.) cans refrigerated biscuits
1	(3-oz.) pkg. butterscotch pudding mix
¼	cup butter
¼	cup brown sugar

Party prep: I recommend making these on the morning you are serving them. They are best served warm with Cream Cheese Glaze (next page). If you have to make them ahead of time, store them in a muffin pan, covered, in the refrigerator. Heat them directly in the muffin tin before removing and serving.

Styling ideas: While I don't bake these in muffin liners, they are cute served in them! Place the monkey bread muffin directly in the liner and serve warm topped with Cream Cheese Glaze. This way, you can match the muffins with any color or theme!

Directions:

• Preheat oven to 350 degrees.

• Open biscuits and use a sharp knife to cut each biscuit into about 8 pieces.

• Toss biscuit pieces in dry butterscotch pudding mix.

• Lightly grease a muffin pan and place coated biscuit pieces directly in without using liners.

• Melt butter and stir in brown sugar.

• Spoon mixture over each muffin.

• Bake for 14–16 minutes.

• Remove from oven and allow to cool enough to handle before removing them from the muffin pan.

Cream Cheese Glaze

Makes about ½ cup

Ingredients

2   oz. cream cheese, room temperature

¼   cup + 1 Tbsp. powdered sugar

2   Tbsp. milk

Party prep: Glaze can be made up to 1 day ahead of time and stored in the refrigerator.

Styling ideas: Adjusting the amount of milk you use will give you more control over the desired look. Add more milk to create a cream cheese drizzle and less to create a spread or to pipe a certain shape. Strawberry cream cheese can be substituted or food coloring can be added for a cute pop of color!

Directions:

• Combine cream cheese and powdered sugar and stir until incorporated.

• Add milk until desired consistency is reached.

Breakfast & Brunch

Southwest Mini Egg Frittatas

Makes about 12 frittatas

Ingredients

8   eggs

½   cup milk

2   Tbsp. salsa

1   (4-oz.) can chopped green chilies

1   tsp. salt

½   tsp. pepper

1½   cups cooked spicy ground sausage

2   cups shredded cheddar cheese

Party prep: These can be made up to 2 days in advance and stored in the refrigerator. Warm in the oven or microwave before serving.

Styling ideas: While these are perfectly cute on their own, stacking them and adding a little mini flag to the top can't hurt, right?

Directions:

• Preheat oven to 350 degrees and lightly grease a muffin pan.

• Whisk together eggs, milk, salsa, green chilies, and salt in a large bowl.

• Fill muffin pan with egg mixture.

• Top each muffin with pepper, sausage, and cheese.

• Bake for 20–24 minutes or until egg is cooked through to the center.

• Remove frittatas from the pan when they are cool enough to handle. Serve warm.

Breakfast & Brunch

Cinnamon French Toast Dippers

Makes about 5 servings

Ingredients

4 eggs

¾ cup heavy cream

½ tsp. cinnamon

1 Tbsp. honey

8 slices buttermilk bread

syrup

Party prep: These can be made up to 1 day in advance. Store in an airtight container in the refrigerator until ready to serve. Reheat in the oven prior to serving.

Styling ideas: These dippers are served perfectly in a fry box! Place one serving of dippers into the fry box and serve with a side of syrup in a wax baking cup. You can get fry boxes in all shapes, sizes, and patterns to fit any theme or color. See the resources list (p. 175) for the one seen in this photo.

Directions:

• Whisk together eggs, cream, cinnamon, and honey in a shallow dish.

• Heat a griddle or pan to medium-high temperature.

• Coat each slice of bread in egg mixture.

• Cook slices on the griddle until both sides are browned and cooked through.

• Remove from the heat and allow to cool.

• Cut each slice into strips for easy dipping and serve with syrup.

Apricot Cherry Scones

Makes about 6 large scones

Ingredients

- 2 cups flour
- ⅓ cup + 1 Tbsp. sugar, divided
- 2 tsp. baking powder
- ½ tsp. salt
- ½ cup sour cream
- ¼ cup + 2 Tbsp. heavy cream, divided
- 1 egg
- 2 tsp. cherry extract
- 8 Tbsp. butter
- 1 cup dry chopped cherry and apricot pieces
- 2 Tbsp. apricot spread
- 1 Tbsp. powdered sugar
- 2 Tbsp. water

Party prep: These can be made up to 1 day in advance and stored in the refrigerator in an airtight container. I recommend making them fresh, though.

Styling ideas: Scones are so girly to me! I love serving them at tea parties and breakfast or brunch parties. Serve with the apricot topping on the side and allow the girls to drizzle their own scones.

Directions:

- Preheat the oven to 400 degrees.

- Whisk together the flour, ⅓ cup sugar, baking powder, and salt in a large bowl.

- In a small bowl, whisk together the sour cream, ¼ cup heavy cream, egg, and cherry extract.

- Cut the butter into small cubes and, using your hands or a pastry cutter, incorporate the butter into the flour mixture until the dough is coarse and in small pieces.*

- Add in the dry fruit pieces and stir to combine.

- Add the wet ingredients to the large bowl and stir gently with a fork to combine—it is important to not overmix! Stop mixing when the dough has loosely come together. It does not have to be perfectly mixed; there may be dry places, which is okay.

- Line a sheet pan with parchment paper and turn the dough out of the bowl onto the center of the pan. Use your hands to form a 6- to 8-inch circle.

- Use a dough scraper or a sharp knife to cut the circle into 6 wedges. Carefully slide the wedges apart to give them room to cook.

- Brush the top of each scone with heavy cream and top with a sprinkling of sugar.

- Cook for 30 minutes or until the edges are just golden brown.

- While cooking, mix apricot spread, powdered sugar, and water to create your topping. Once the scones are removed from the oven and still warm, top them with a drizzle of this topping.

  Tip: Placing your butter in the freezer for a few minutes will help keep its shape while cutting it into cubes.

Breakfast & Brunch

Pancake Breakfast Skewers

Makes 12–14 servings

Ingredients

1	(32-oz.) pkg. pancake mix
1½	cups blueberries
1½	cups raspberries
1	(12-oz.) pkg. mini powdered donuts

Party prep: The pancakes can be made up to a day ahead of time and stored in the refrigerator. Reheat before assembling skewers.

Styling ideas: These were a big hit! The girls loved the presentation with the cute ribbon bow at the top, which can be adjusted to any color scheme of your party. I served them on a platter with the fruit scattered around and any remaining fruit or donuts served on the side.

Directions:

- Make pancake batter according to package directions.

- Heat griddle or pan over medium-high heat.

- Make circular pancakes that are various sizes, from 1½ inches to 3 inches in diameter.

- Allow pancakes to cool enough to handle. Stack 3–4 pancakes of varying sizes with the largest at the bottom and the smallest at the top.

- Slide a large blueberry about halfway onto a wooden skewer, followed by a raspberry and then a mini donut.

- Place the skewer into the stack of pancakes. Slide the fruit and donut to adjust for the height.

Breakfast & Brunch

Chocolate Cake Waffles

Makes 6–8 servings

Ingredients

- 1 (18-oz.) box chocolate cake mix
- 2 cups sliced strawberries
- 4 Tbsp. powdered sugar, divided
- 2 cups heavy cream
- 1 Tbsp. cocoa powder
- 4 oz. melted chocolate
- ½ cup mini chocolate chips

Party prep: The waffles and chocolate whipped cream can be made up to 2 days ahead of time and stored airtight in the refrigerator. Heat waffles before serving, and prepare strawberries about 20 minutes before serving.

Styling ideas: I love the pop of color that the strawberries give to the plate! I serve this family style and allow the girls to control the amount of topping for their waffles. This recipe can be adapted using different cake mix flavors as well. I have made fun birthday cake waffles with sprinkles and German chocolate waffles—the possibilities are endless!

Directions:

- Lightly grease and heat a waffle iron. Make chocolate cake batter according to directions.

- Cook waffles using cake batter on waffle iron according to manufacturer's instructions.

- In a small bowl, mix together strawberries and 2 tablespoons powdered sugar and set aside to macerate.

- Combine heavy cream, 2 tablespoons powdered sugar, and cocoa powder in a stand mixer with the whisk attachment (or use a medium bowl and a hand mixer).

- Whip until soft peaks begin to form.

- Add cooled melted chocolate and continue whipping to combine.

- Serve waffles warm with a heaping topping of chocolate whipped cream, strawberries, and mini chocolate chips.

Blackberry, Almond & Honey Yogurt Parfaits

Makes 6–8 servings

Ingredients

24	oz. plain Greek yogurt
1½	cups granola
¾	cup honey roasted almond slices
12	oz. blackberries
6	Tbsp. honey

*P*arty prep: These should be assembled as close to serving as possible to maintain the integrity of the texture.

*S*tyling ideas: Layer parfaits in tall skinny glasses to best show each individual layer. Be sure to spread each layer evenly around the diameter of the glass so it can be seen from all angles. Use tall skinny spoons so the girls can get multiple layers with each bite! To style, I used purples in the décor and the flowers to bring out the color of the blackberries in the parfait.

Directions:

- Layer yogurt in the bottom of the glasses.

- Add a layer of granola, then almonds, then blackberries, and then a squeeze of honey.

- Repeat as many layers as your glasses will hold.

Tip: How do you avoid getting yogurt on the sides of the glass? It's easy—place the yogurt in a plastic bag, snip the corner, and pipe it right into the bottom!

Breakfast & Brunch

Fruity Cereal Pops

Makes 6 servings

Ingredients

4	Tbsp. butter
15	oz. marshmallows
6	cups fruity cereal
4	oz. melted white chocolate or candy coating

 Party prep: These can be made in advance up to 2 days ahead of time and kept in an airtight container separated by wax paper.

 Styling ideas: This recipe is adaptable to lots of party color schemes simply by switching up the cereal! Adding little ribbons to the popsicle sticks gives them that extra girly touch.

Directions:

- Melt the butter in a medium saucepan. Set heat to low.

- Stir in marshmallows and melt on low heat.

- Once the marshmallows are completely melted, remove from heat and stir in cereal until coated.

- Scoop out cereal, dividing it into 6 even piles on parchment paper.

- Allow to cool slightly and then mold the piles into popsicle shapes.

- Place a popsicle stick into each treat.

- Once the treats are fully cooled, drizzle melted white chocolate or candy coating over the top.

Fruit Pastries

Makes 8 pastries

Ingredients

4	oz. cream cheese, room temperature

4 oz. cream cheese, room temperature

¼ cup butter, room temperature

1¾ cups powdered sugar

½ tsp. vanilla bean extract

18 oz. puff pastry sheets, thawed

½ cup fresh berries (blueberries, raspberries, strawberries, etc.)

Party prep: These can be made in advance up to 2 days ahead of time and kept in an airtight container separated by wax paper. Allow to come to room temperature or warm them slightly before serving.

Styling ideas: These are great for breakfast and brunch parties. They are a favorite in our household. I usually serve them in a bread basket or a bowl with a napkin or cute fabric lining the bowl. The fabric is a great opportunity to coordinate with colors or themes at your event.

Directions:

• Preheat oven to 400 degrees.

• Blend cream cheese and butter together.

• On low speed, add powdered sugar 1 cup at a time.

• Add vanilla extract and blend on high for 2–3 minutes. Set aside.

• Cut the pastry sheets into 8 squares and press to seal any seams.

• Take one of the squares and fold each point into the center. Repeat step for all squares.

- Place a dollop of the cream cheese mixture in the center of each square.

- Add a few berries to the center of the cream cheese mixture.

- Optional: Brush with egg wash to give it a shiny crust.

- Bake for 12–16 minutes.

Breakfast & Brunch

Light Lunch

Entertain your guests during the lunch hour with these delicious and light recipes. Great for midday parties, afternoon tea, or just lunch with the girls!

Orange Chicken Salad Sandwiches

Makes about 10 servings

Ingredients

- 4 cups shredded or cubed chicken
- ¾ cup coarsely chopped cashews
- ¾ cup dried cranberries
- 1 (11-oz.) can mandarin oranges
- ½ cup diced celery
- 2 Tbsp. frozen orange juice
- 1 (3-oz.) container orange yogurt
- ½ tsp. curry
- ½ cup mayonnaise
- 10–12 large sandwich rolls

Party prep: The chicken salad can be made up to 1 day in advance and stored in an airtight container. Do not place the chicken salad in the rolls for longer than 3 hours in the refrigerator or the rolls will get soggy.

Styling ideas: It's easy to dress these up with a fun little flag! I took decorative washi tape and folded it over a wooden toothpick. It's simple but also a great way to add a punch of color to your food. Prepare the toothpicks ahead of time and place in the sandwiches right before serving.

Directions:

- Combine the chicken, cashews, dried cranberries, mandarin oranges, and celery in a large bowl.
- Add the frozen orange juice into a small bowl and allow it to thaw.
- Once thawed, add the yogurt, curry, and mayonnaise and whisk to combine.
- Pour yogurt mixture over the chicken and toss to coat.
- Cut rolls in half and fill with chicken salad.
- Serve immediately or store in the refrigerator for up to 3 hours.

Light Lunch

Wedge Salad Skewers

Makes about 10 servings

Ingredients

1	head iceberg lettuce
3	cups cherry tomatoes
½	cup crumbled blue cheese
½	cup crumbled bacon
1	cup blue cheese dressing

Party prep: This is one of those recipes you have to prepare on the day of the event. Salads don't keep well, and cutting a salad with a knife tends to make it brown on the edges (not so pretty). I recommend having all of the ingredients ready to go and making this right before the party starts. It can be kept in the fridge for about 30 minutes before serving but is best when served immediately.

Styling ideas: The drizzle of the dressing, the pop of red from the tomatoes, the crumbled blue cheese, and the crumbled bacon make this look elegant. You could always add a bit of flair to the skewers with washi tape or ribbon on the ends.

Directions:

- Cut the lettuce head into quarter wedges. Then cut each in half again to create 8 thin wedges. Starting from the edge, cut sections to create mini wedges.

- Slide the lettuce wedge onto a skewer followed by a cherry tomato. Repeat until the skewer is filled. Repeat with all skewers.

- Arrange skewers horizontally on a platter and sprinkle with crumbled blue cheese and bacon.

- Drizzle blue cheese dressing over the top.

- Serve immediately.

Grapefruit Chicken Salad

Makes about 6 servings

Ingredients

3	large grapefruits
½	head iceberg lettuce, chopped
1	cup sliced jicama
2	cups cooked cubed chicken
1	cup Citrus Poppy Seed Dressing (next page)
¼	cup toasted sesame seeds
¾	cup crispy chow mein noodles

Party prep: You can prep the grapefruit, jicama, and chicken 1 day ahead of time kept in an airtight container in the refrigerator. Toss the salad and dressing together on the day of the party but serve immediately or store up to 30 minutes in the refrigerator. Garnish right before serving.

Styling ideas: When possible, use your ingredients as serving pieces. Serve this recipe in a halved grapefruit. Simply scrape away the segment membranes from the grapefruit peel and you have a bowl!

Directions:

- Cut each grapefruit in half horizontally. Use a paring knife to cut out the segments of grapefruit.

- Toss together the grapefruit, lettuce, jicama, chicken, and dressing.

- Serve garnished with toasted sesame seeds and crispy chow mein noodles.

Citrus Poppy Seed Dressing

Makes about 1½ cups

Ingredients

- ¼ cup fresh grapefruit juice
- ¼ cup red wine vinegar
- ½ cup oil
- ½ cup sugar
- ¼ tsp. salt
- 2 tsp. toasted sesame seeds
- ½ tsp. sesame oil

Party prep: This can be made and stored in the refrigerator for up to 5 days.

Styling ideas: Try serving your salad dressing in a mason jar! This dressing needs to be shaken before it is served, so a mason jar is perfect and adds a personalized feel to the table.

Directions:

- Add ingredients together and whisk to combine.
- Shake before serving.

Light Lunch

Greek Tortellini Salad

Makes about 8 servings

Ingredients

1½ cups halved cherry tomatoes

1 (16-oz.) pkg. cooked cheese tortellini

1 green pepper, diced

¼ red onion, diced

3 oz. olives, diced

1 cup chopped parsley

1 cup crumbled feta cheese

¾ cup Greek dressing

Party prep: This can be made up to 3 days in advance if kept in the refrigerator.

Styling ideas: I love this salad! It is a big hit every time I serve it. Brown paper trays and bamboo utensils complement each other perfectly and are an adorable way to allow your guests to get exactly the amount they want.

Directions:

- Combine all ingredients in a large bowl and toss to coat.

- Chill for 1 hour and then serve.

Light Lunch

Grilled Cheese Hearts with Roasted Tomato & Cauliflower Soup

Makes about 6 servings

Ingredients

7	roma tomatoes; washed, cored, and cut in half
1	small onion, roughly chopped
¾	cauliflower head, roughly chopped
2	garlic cloves
¼	cup olive oil
8	oz. chicken stock
1	tsp. adobo seasoning
½	tsp. cumin
⅛	tsp. ground cayenne pepper
2	bay leaves
½	tsp. salt
½	tsp. pepper
¾	cup half-and-half
3	Tbsp. butter, room temperature
12	slices bread
2	cups shredded cheddar cheese

Party prep: The soup can be made up to 4 days in advance if kept in the refrigerator. The grilled cheese hearts are best served fresh but can be made the day before and reheated before serving if needed.

Styling ideas: Serve the soup in a skinny glass so that the grilled cheese hearts can balance on each serving!

Directions:

- Preheat oven to 425 degrees.

- Spread tomatoes, onion, cauliflower, and garlic cloves on a baking sheet.

- Drizzle with olive oil.

- Bake for 25–30 minutes or until roasted and browned.

- Remove baking sheet and allow to cool enough to handle.

- Place all of the roasted vegetables into a blender or food processor and blend until smooth. Pour into a saucepan on medium heat.

- Add chicken stock, adobo seasoning, cumin, cayenne pepper, bay leaves, salt, and pepper. Bring to a simmer.

- Simmer on low for 10 minutes.

- Turn off the heat, remove bay leaves, and add half-and-half. Stir to incorporate.

- Set aside and keep warm if serving immediately.

- Turn on a griddle to high heat.

- Spread butter on one side of the bread slices and sandwich shredded cheese in the middle of 2 bread slices with the butter facing outward.

- Place the sandwich on the griddle until golden brown. Flip. Remove when golden brown on the other side.

- While still warm, press a cookie cutter into the center of the sandwich. I used a heart cookie cutter, but any shape will work. Repeat steps for all grilled cheese sandwiches.

- Serve warm soup and grilled cheese together.

Light Lunch

Entrées

If you are entertaining around dinnertime,
these are fun and tasty recipes every girl will love!

Parmesan Chicken Fingers

Makes about 8 servings

Ingredients

1	Tbsp. vegetable oil
1	cup heavy cream
1	cup panko bread crumbs
½	cup grated parmesan cheese
½	cup shredded parmesan cheese
¼	tsp. salt
¼	tsp. pepper
1	lb. chicken tenderloins

Party prep: These can be made up to 3 days in advance if kept in the refrigerator. Reheat in a 350-degree oven for about 5 minutes before serving.

Styling ideas: These are great served with Honey Mustard Sauce for dipping (next page). I like to serve these in individual bundles so they are ready to grab! Form a cone with decorative wax paper. Fill it with 3–4 chicken fingers and stack on a platter for your guests!

Directions:

- Preheat oven to 450 degrees.

- In a shallow dish, combine oil and cream.

- In a second shallow dish, combine bread crumbs, both types of cheese, salt, and pepper.

- Dredge the chicken in the wet mixture and then toss in the dry mixture.

- Place on a baking sheet.

- Bake for 15–18 minutes or until chicken is cooked through and coating is golden brown.

Honey Mustard Sauce

Makes about 1 cup

Ingredients

- ½ cup mayonnaise
- ¼ cup yellow mustard
- 2 Tbsp. honey
- 2 tsp. lemon juice
- ½ tsp. garlic powder
- ½ tsp. onion powder
- ¼ tsp. salt
- ¼ tsp. paprika

 Party prep: This can be made up to 3 days ahead of time if kept in the refrigerator. It is best served at room temperature.

 Styling ideas: This is great served with Parmesan Chicken Fingers (previous page). I use cute little dipping bowls to serve the dip!

Directions:

- Combine ingredients in a small bowl.

Entrées

Barbecue Chicken Pizza Pinwheels

Makes about 5 servings

Ingredients

1 (12-oz.) pkg. refrigerated pizza dough

½ cup barbecue sauce

½ cup finely chopped cooked chicken

1 cup mozzarella cheese

Party prep: These can be made up to 3 days ahead of time if kept in the refrigerator. Reheat them in the oven prior to serving.

Styling ideas: These are pizza pinwheels—so why not serve them to look like that? To display them, place a Styrofoam block into a galvanized bucket with something to weigh down the bottom (it can get top heavy). Skewer through the pizza circle and secure the skewer upright into the Styrofoam. Cover the top of the bucket with shredded paper to coordinate with your party colors and theme!

Directions:

- Preheat oven according to pizza dough directions.

- Roll out pizza dough on a lightly floured surface into a rectangle shape.

- Cover with barbecue sauce, chicken, and cheese.

- Roll one of the longer sides toward the center and to the other side.

- Use a very sharp knife to cut 1½-inch rounds.

- Transfer the rounds to a baking sheet with the flat side down, showing the spiral. Reshape into a circle and bake according to package directions or until golden brown.

Entrées

Sweet Pulled Pork Sliders with Cilantro Coleslaw

Makes about 12–15 servings

Ingredients

1	lb. pork (boneless shoulder or tenderloin)
1	can Coca-Cola
1	cup brown sugar
1	tsp. garlic powder
1	tsp. onion powder
1	(4-oz.) can green chilies
1	(10-oz.) can red enchilada sauce
4	cups premade coleslaw mix
1	cup Cilantro Dip (p. 18)
12–15	sandwich rolls
3	avocados, sliced

Party prep: The pork can be made up to 4 days in advance while the coleslaw can be made 1 day in advance if kept in the refrigerator. Slice the avocado and assemble sandwiches right before serving.

Styling ideas: Since these have to be assembled right before serving, this recipe is a great opportunity for a build-your-own station. This is a favorite at our household. You could always add a bit of flair to the toothpicks with washi tape or ribbon on the ends as well.

Directions:

- Place the pork into a slow cooker and cover halfway with water.

- Cook on low for 3–4 hours or on high for 7–8 hours.

- Drain pork and shred meat. Replace back into the slow cooker.

- Add Coca-Cola, brown sugar, garlic powder, onion powder, green chilies, and enchilada sauce. Cook for another 30 minutes on low.

- Mix together coleslaw mix and Cilantro Dip.

- Slice sandwich rolls and put shredded pork inside. Top with the coleslaw and slices of avocado. Serve immediately.

Pineapple Chicken Kabobs

Makes about 8 servings

Ingredients

1   lb. chicken tenders

1   cup teriyaki sauce, divided

1   fresh pineapple

1   cup Satay Sauce (next page)

Party prep: The pineapple can be cut up to 2 days in advance, and skewers can be prepared the day before the party if kept in the refrigerator. I recommend grilling the day of the party.

Styling ideas: Use brightly colored yellow napkins and party accessories to bring out the pop of yellow in the pineapple! The look of the grill marks makes this a great dish to serve at any rustic party.

Directions:

• Marinate the chicken tenders in teriyaki sauce for 30 minutes in the refrigerator, but set 3 tablespoons of teriyaki sauce aside.

• Cut the pineapple into bite-size pieces.

• Preheat the grill to medium-high.

• Skewer pineapple and chicken tenders on skewers and brush with remaining teriyaki sauce.

• Grill for 4 minutes on each side or until chicken is cooked through.

• Serve warm with Satay Sauce for dipping.

Satay Sauce

Makes about 3 cups

Ingredients

1	(13-oz.) can coconut milk
½	cup peanut butter
2	Tbsp. soy sauce
2	tsp. chili sauce
½	tsp. garlic powder
½	tsp. onion powder
1	Tbsp. sesame oil
2½	Tbsp. brown sugar

Party prep: This can be made up to 5 days in advance if kept in the refrigerator. Reheat in a saucepan when ready to serve.

Styling ideas: This recipe makes a lot, but in addition to being a dipping sauce, it can be served over rice or noodles as well. I serve this as a dipping sauce with the Pineapple Chicken Kabobs (previous page).

Directions:

• Combine all the ingredients in a saucepan over medium-low heat. Simmer for 5–10 minutes and serve warm.

Entrées

Drinks

It wouldn't be a party without some fun drinks! Here are a few nonalcoholic party drinks that can be enjoyed by girls of any age.

Raspberry Mint Lemonade

Makes about 8 servings

Ingredients

6	oz. raspberries
1	cup + 2 Tbsp. lemon juice, divided
2	Tbsp. julienned mint
2	cups warm water
1	cup sugar
2	cups cold water

Party prep: Lemonade will keep in the refrigerator for up to 4 days. The raspberry mint cubes will keep in the freezer for up to 3 months. Keep raspberry cubes separate from the lemonade until serving.

Styling ideas: Garnish with a fresh sprig of mint or a slice of lemon and use cute striped straws! This recipe can be adapted to many different flavors and colors to fit your party color scheme.

Directions:

- Blend raspberries and 2 tablespoons lemon juice.

- Press this mixture through a sieve to remove seeds.

- Mix with mint and place into an ice cube tray. Freeze until ready to serve.

- In a pitcher, combine warm water and sugar together until sugar has dissolved.

- Add one cup of lemon juice and cold water to the pitcher.

- Chill until ready to serve.

- Serve lemonade in glasses with the raspberry mint ice cubes.

Drinks

Strawberry Kiwi Layered Drinks

Makes about 6 drinks

Ingredients

6   cups strawberry kiwi punch (green, higher sugar content)

6   cups fruit punch (red, lower sugar content)

Party prep: This drink should be made right before serving. The drinks will stay separated for about twenty minutes.

Styling ideas: This concept can be applied to many different color schemes and flavors. Just be sure the sugar content varies enough to keep the juice separated. Using cute straws and garnishes are an easy way to dress this up for a party.

Directions:

- Fill your cups to the brim with ice.

- Slowly pour the strawberry kiwi punch into the glass until it is about half full.

- Slowly pour the fruit punch into the glass until it is full.

Fruit Smoothies

Makes about 3 smoothie servings

Mango Pineapple

Ingredients

6	oz. orange yogurt
1	mango, peeled and pitted
½	banana
¾	cup cut fresh pineapple
¼	cup orange juice
1	cup ice

Strawberry Banana

Ingredients

½	banana
5	strawberries
6	oz. strawberry yogurt
¼	cup milk
1	cup ice

Kiwi Coconut

Ingredients

2	kiwifruits, peeled
6	oz. piña colada yogurt
½	banana
¼	cup coconut milk
1	cup ice

Directions for Fruit Smoothies:

- Place all ingredients in a blender and mix until smooth.

- Pour into glasses and top with Coconut Whipped Cream (below).

Party prep: These should be made right before serving.

Styling ideas: Use coordinating fruit to garnish the side of the glass and cute straws to match!

Coconut Whipped Cream

Makes about 2 cups

Ingredients

| 1 | (13-oz.) can coconut milk |
| 3 | Tbsp. powdered sugar |

Party prep: This can be made the day before the party and refrigerated until serving.

Styling ideas: This is the perfect complement to any smoothie (above), pie, or ice cream!

Directions:

- Refrigerate the can of coconut milk overnight.

- Without shaking the can, open the top and remove the solid part.

- Place the solid coconut into a bowl and whip on high until peaks form.

- Add the powdered sugar and whip to combine.

Drinks

Raspberry Party Punch

Makes 20–25 servings

Ingredients

¾	quart raspberry sherbet
1	(12–fl. oz.) can frozen lemonade mix, thawed
3	cups water
2	liters lemon-lime soda

Party prep: This should be made the day of the party right before your guests arrive.

Styling ideas: Garnish with lemon slices in the glasses as well as in the punch bowl.

Directions:

- Scoop the frozen raspberry sherbet into a punch bowl.

- Combine the thawed lemonade mixture and water. Pour this over the sherbet.

- Pour the soda into the punch bowl and serve.

Drinks

Fruity Italian Sodas

Makes as many servings as needed

Ingredients

1   part fruit syrup

2   parts club soda

1   part half-and-half

*P*arty prep: This should be made during the party per the guests' flavor requests.

*S*tyling ideas: Use coordinating fruit to garnish the sides of the glasses and cute straws to match. Serve flavors with colors that coordinate to your color scheme.

Directions:

- Fill a glass with ice and pour fruit syrup into glass.
- Fill the glass with club soda and top it off with half-and-half.

Flavored Hot Chocolate Spoons

Makes 10 servings

Ingredients

6   oz. assorted chocolate chips

3   oz. assorted toppings

Party prep: These can be made up to 3 days in advance if kept in the refrigerator. Allow to come to room temperature before serving.

Styling ideas: You can choose from so many flavor options for this. Here I have used coconut, peppermint, butterscotch, dark chocolate, and toffee. I love using party printables to tie everything together. I used printable patterned paper to cover the handle of the spoon as well as washi tape and mini printable circles at the top. Serve this with straws that coordinate with the printables. Serve with Hot Chocolate (p. 104) and Whipped Cream Shapes (p. 106).

Directions:

- Melt the chocolate in a microwave-safe bowl for 1 minute on low power. Stir and repeat for thirty-second increments until the chocolate is smooth and melted.

- Place a dollop of chocolate on the end of the spoon.

- While it is still melted, press toppings into the chocolate.

- Allow to set at room temperature or in the refrigerator. Be sure to keep the spoon level during this step.

- Serve with hot chocolate. Have your guests choose the flavor spoon they would like and stir it into their hot chocolate.

Drinks

Hot Chocolate

Makes about 8 servings

Ingredients

¾	cup unsweetened cocoa powder
1½	cups sugar
½	tsp. salt
1	cup water
1	tsp. vanilla bean paste
7	cups milk
½	cup cream

Party prep: Make hot chocolate before the event and keep it warm on the stove.

Styling ideas: Serve with Flavored Hot Chocolate Spoons (p. 103) and Whipped Cream Shapes (p. 106)!

Directions:

- Combine cocoa powder, sugar, salt, water, and vanilla bean paste in a medium saucepan and bring to a simmer. Stir and simmer for about 1 minute.

- Turn the heat to low, allow to cool slightly, and stir in milk.

- When combined, stir in the cream, remove from heat, and serve.

Whipped Cream Shapes

Makes about 25 one-inch shapes

Ingredients

8   oz. whipped cream
     topping

Party prep: If you would like to cut the shapes out ahead of time, just leave them on the sheet pan and place them back in the freezer until the party. They should be served immediately after being removed from the freezer.

Styling ideas: Serve with Flavored Hot Chocolate Spoons (p. 103) and Hot Chocolate (p. 104). Create whatever shape you desire based on your party theme!

Directions:

• Line a baking sheet with plastic wrap.

• Spread whipped cream topping into the pan so that it is about one inch thick. (Note: this may only be a portion of your baking sheet.)

• Freeze for a minimum of 4 hours.

• Remove the pan from the freezer and use cookie cutters to create desired shapes.

Cookies, Bars & Pies

Everyone loves a sweet treat at a party! My favorite part
of party planning is choosing the desserts I will serve. These are
some of the favorite recipes that my guests have enjoyed.

Individual Fruit Pizzas

Makes 10 servings

Ingredients

8	oz. cream cheese, room temperature
½	cup butter, room temperature
3½	cups powdered sugar
1	tsp. vanilla bean extract
10	sugar cookies, 4–5 inches in diameter
8	oz. fresh fruit of choice

Party prep: The cream cheese frosting will keep in the refrigerator for up to 4 days. Bring it to room temperature before spreading on the cookies. Prepare right before guests arrive or make on-the-spot custom pizzas per your guests' requests!

Styling ideas: You can use any fruit for this concept—pick things that are in season and coordinate with the colors and feel of your event. You can even branch out beyond fruit and incorporate chocolate, honey, nuts, and more. Setting up a "make your own" station with small bowls of toppings can be a fun activity at your party!

Directions:

- Blend cream cheese and butter together.

- On low speed, add powdered sugar 1 cup at a time.

- Add vanilla extract and blend on high for 2–3 minutes.

- Spread frosting over the sugar cookies and top with fresh fruit.

Cookies, Bars & Pies

Peanut Butter Caramel Shortbread Bars

Makes 9–12 servings

Ingredients

1	cup butter, room temperature
½	cup sugar
¾	cup powdered sugar
1	Tbsp. vanilla bean paste
2¼	cups flour
7	oz. caramel candy melts
3	Tbsp. heavy cream
7	oz. peanut butter chips

 Party prep: These can be made up to 2 days in advance. Store in the refrigerator but allow it to come to room temperature before serving.

 Styling ideas: These would be great wrapped in some adorable wax paper and tied up with twine!

Directions:

- Preheat oven to 325 degrees.

- Combine butter, sugar, powdered sugar, and vanilla bean paste until smooth and light.

- On low speed, add the flour ½ cup at a time until dough forms.

- Grease a 9×9 pan and press ¾ of the dough evenly into the pan.

- Refrigerate the remaining dough.

- Bake for 15–18 minutes or until edges are lightly browned.

- In a small saucepan, combine caramel and heavy cream over low heat. Stir until melted.

- Pour over top of the baked shortbread.

- Sprinkle caramel with peanut butter chips.

- Remove the remaining dough from the refrigerator and crumble over the top.

- Bake at 325 degrees for another 20 minutes or until golden brown.

- Remove and allow to completely cool to room temperature before cutting into bars.

Pink French Macarons with Chocolate Buttercream

Makes 2 dozen filled macaron cookies

Ingredients

110	g almond flour
200	g powdered sugar
100	g egg whites, room temperature
¼	tsp. cream of tartar
35	g superfine sugar
	pink food coloring
1	cup unsalted butter, softened
3½	cups sifted powdered sugar
1	cup cocoa powder
1½	tsp. almond extract
2	Tbsp. water
¼	tsp. salt

Party prep: Filled macarons can be stored in an airtight container for up to a week. They are best after about 12 hours in the fridge and warmed to room temperature.

Styling ideas: Macarons are the new cupcake! They are trendy and a fabulous delicate treat to satisfy your party guests. You can color them to fit any color scheme and you can also pipe them into interesting shapes using different templates (see p. 176 for more on macarons).

Directions:

- Measure out all ingredients and set aside.

- Prepare baking sheets by lining them with parchment paper.

- Sift the powdered sugar and almond flour together 2–3 times through a sieve and set aside. Discard large almond pieces that remain in sieve.

- Place the egg whites in a large bowl or in stand mixer with wire whisk attachment. Whisk on low speed until egg whites become foamy. Add the pinch of cream of tartar. Continue to whisk on medium-low until soft peaks form. Slowly add in the superfine sugar.

- Turn mixer to medium-high and continue to whip until peaks begin to form. Slow down speed and check egg whites periodically until you reach a stiff meringue. Add pink food coloring toward the end of whisking to desired color.

- Sift one-third of the almond flour and powdered sugar mixture through the sieve and into the meringue. Fold the dry mixture into the meringue. Repeat with the remaining almond flour and powdered sugar mixture. Once all of the dry ingredients are incorporated, the batter will be thick and have a dull shine. Continue to fold. As you do so, the batter will loosen. Stop folding when the batter has a glossy sheen and a lava-like consistency and until it falls in a ribbon-like manner off the spatula.

- Transfer the batter into a large pastry bag fitted with a round tip. Pipe 1½-inch rounds on the parchment paper. (Follow template if needed—see p. 176 for macaron templates.)

- When all of the rounds are piped on the parchment, rap the sheet pans evenly on work surface a few times to release any trapped air and to encourage the batter to spread evenly. (If used, remove templates from below your parchment paper carefully.) Let the batter rest at room temperature for 20–40 minutes.

- Preheat oven to 350 degrees. Reduce temperature to 300 degrees and bake one sheet at a time for 10 minutes, rotating the pan halfway through. Remove from oven and allow to cool for 5 minutes. Transfer to a wire cooling rack.

- In a medium bowl, mix butter and sifted powdered sugar together on low speed.

- Add cocoa powder and continue to mix on low speed.

- Add almond extract, water, and salt. Mix on high speed until smooth.

- Match up similar-sized shells and pipe chocolate buttercream on one shell. Sandwich together and serve.

Cherry & White Chocolate Chip Cookies

Makes about 18 cookies

Ingredients

1	cup butter, room temperature
1	cup sugar
1	cup brown sugar
2	eggs
1	tsp. almond extract
1	tsp. cherry extract
3	cups flour
1	tsp. salt
1	tsp. baking soda
6	oz. dried cherries
6	oz. white chocolate chips

Party prep: These can be made up to 2 days in advance. Keep in an airtight container separated by wax paper.

Styling ideas: These would be great wrapped in some adorable patterned wax paper tied up with twine!

Directions:

- Preheat oven to 375 degrees.

- Combine butter, sugar, and brown sugar until light and creamy.

- Add the eggs, almond extract, and cherry extract and mix until combined.

- In a separate bowl, combine flour, salt, baking soda, cherries, and chocolate chips.

- Incorporate the dry ingredients into the wet ingredients one cup at a time. Don't overmix.

- Scoop cookie dough onto a baking sheet at desired size (I usually do a heaping tablespoon).

- Bake for 7–9 minutes or until golden brown around the edges.

Raspberry Chocolate Hazelnut Cookie Cups

Makes 10 servings

Ingredients

1   (16-oz.) pkg. refrigerated sugar cookie dough

4   oz. raspberry preserves

6   oz. chocolate hazelnut spread

2   oz. fresh raspberries

Party prep: These can be made up to 1 day in advance if kept in the refrigerator and up to 1 week in advance if kept in the freezer. Allow to come to room temperature or slightly chilled before serving.

Styling ideas: These are the most delightful little treats! They are tiny enough to be a one- or two-bite dessert, so all you need are cute napkins for your guests.

Directions:

- Preheat oven to 350 degrees.

- Cut 1-ounce rounds of sugar cookie dough and press each round into a cavity of a mini muffin pan.

- Bake for 15–20 minutes.

- Remove cookies from oven. While still warm, use a spoon to press the dough against the side of the muffin cavities, creating small cup shapes.

- Once cooled, remove from muffin pan.

- Place a small dollop of raspberry preserves into the bottom of each sugar cookie cup followed by a spoonful of chocolate hazelnut spread to fill the cavity.

- Top with a fresh raspberry.

- Serve room temperature or slightly chilled.

Cookies, Bars & Pies

Blueberry Mini Pies

Makes about 12 servings

Ingredients

2 cups blueberries

4 tsp. sugar, divided

2 tsp. brown sugar

1 tsp. cornstarch

2 tsp. lemon juice

1 (14-oz.) pkg. piecrust

2 Tbsp. water (optional)

1 egg (optional)

Party prep: These can be made up to 2 days in advance and kept in the refrigerator until the day of the party. Serve at room temperature or warmed.

Styling ideas: These pies are great for a rustic party theme. They can be packaged in cupcake boxes, tied up with twine, and given as party favors. They would also look adorable topped with whipped cream hearts (p. 106).

Directions:

• Preheat oven to 375 degrees.

• Combine blueberries, 3 teaspoons sugar, brown sugar, cornstarch, and lemon juice in a small bowl and toss to coat.

• Unroll piecrust onto a slightly floured surface.

• Use a large circular cookie cutter or biscuit cutter to cut circles out of the piecrust.

• Press the piecrust circles into greased muffin tin cavities. The piecrust does not need to fill the whole cavity—they work best about halfway up the sides. Leave some piecrust remaining for the top.

• Place about 1 tablespoon of blueberry pie mixture onto each pie.

• Use a pizza wheel to cut strips out of remaining piecrust.

- Lattice the strips over the blueberry and seal them to the edges of the crust.

- Mix water and egg in a small bowl to create an egg wash. Brush this over the tops of the pies. (This step is optional.)

- Sprinkle the tops with the remaining teaspoon of sugar.

- Bake for 15–20 minutes.

- Allow pies to cool before removing them from the muffin tin.

Cookies, Bars & Pies

Heart-Shaped Raspberry Hand Pies

Makes about 12 servings

Ingredients

1   cup raspberries

1   tsp. cornstarch

4   tsp. sugar, divided

½   tsp. lemon juice

1   (14-oz.) pkg. piecrust

2   Tbsp. water (optional)

1   egg (optional)

Party prep: These can be made up to 2 days in advance and kept in the refrigerator until the day of the party. Serve at room temperature or warmed.

Styling ideas: These hand pies are great for any rustic party theme. They can be packaged in rustic favor bags, tied up with twine, and given as party favors!

Directions:

• Preheat oven to 375 degrees.

• Combine raspberries, cornstarch, 3 teaspoons sugar, and lemon juice in a bowl.

• Use a fork to smash raspberries and mix ingredients to a coarse consistency.

• Unroll piecrust onto a slightly floured surface.

• Use a large heart-shaped cookie cutter to cut heart shapes out of piecrust.

• Prepare a baking sheet with parchment paper and spread half of the hearts onto it.

• Place a small spoonful of raspberry mixture onto the center of 1 heart.

• Dip your clean fingers into a bowl of water and lightly dampen the edge of the heart shape.

- Take another heart-shaped piecrust and align it with the bottom heart.

- Use your finger to seal edges of the hearts together, creating a pocket for the raspberries.

- Use a toothpick or fork to poke a few holes in top heart and score edges to ensure they are sealed.

- Repeat until all hearts are prepared.

- Mix water and egg in a small bowl to create an egg wash. Brush this over the tops of hearts. (This step is optional.)

- Sprinkle tops with remaining teaspoon of sugar.

- Bake for 15–20 minutes.

Cookies, Bars & Pies

Cookie Dough Brownie Push Pops

Makes 10 Push Pops

Ingredients

1	(19-oz.) pkg. brownie mix
½	cup butter
¼	cup brown sugar
1	Tbsp. sugar
½	cup powdered sugar
½	cup flour
1	pinch of salt
1	Tbsp. milk or water*
1	tsp. vanilla bean extract
¼	cup mini chocolate chips

If using milk, be sure to keep the filling refrigerated until consuming.

Party prep: Brownies and frosting can be made up to 2 days in advance if stored airtight in the refrigerator. Assemble pops on the day of the party.

Styling ideas: Push Pop containers can be used for many different recipes! Choose from countless variations of this concept to coordinate with any party theme and color scheme. To display these, simply cover Styrofoam with tissue paper and stick the push pops in to be held upright. Push Pop containers come with a lid as well, which can also be used to hold them upright. You can dress them up with ribbons, printables, stickers, or glue decorations, directly on the container. They are a great tool to personalize a girly event. (See p. 176 for where to buy treat pop containers.)

Directions:

- Bake brownies according to package directions in a 9×13 pan and set aside to cool.

- Cream butter, brown sugar, and sugar together.

- Add remaining ingredients—except chocolate chips—one at a time and mix until combined to complete your frosting.

- Take a Push Pop container and press the top directly onto the brownie like a cookie cutter. Press the brownie to the bottom of the Push Pop.

- Pipe a layer of cookie dough frosting on top of the brownie.

- Repeat layers until the Push Pop is full. Top with more frosting and sprinkle with mini chocolate chips.

Cakes & Cupcakes

There has to be cake, right? Here are some fun ways
to dress up your cakes and cupcakes for a girly party!

Chocolate Hazelnut Raspberry Cupcakes

Makes about 16 cupcakes

Ingredients

- 1 (18-oz.) pkg. chocolate cake mix

- 4 oz. cream cheese, room temperature

- ¼ cup butter, room temperature

- 1¾ cups powdered sugar

- 1 tsp. vanilla bean extract

- 1 cup chocolate hazelnut spread, divided

- 4 oz. fresh raspberries

Party prep: The cupcakes can be made up to 2 days in advance if kept airtight in the refrigerator and unfrosted. Core, fill, and frost cupcakes at most a few hours before the party.

Styling ideas: There are so many cute cupcake liner options out there. Choose one that is fun and fits your theme or color scheme! I like to bake my cupcakes with one liner and display them with an additional liner on the outside to really have the color pop.

Directions:

- Make chocolate cupcakes according to package directions. Set aside to cool.

- Combine cream cheese, butter, powdered sugar, vanilla, and ½ cup chocolate hazelnut spread in a mixer until smooth and creamy.

- Core cupcakes and fill the middle with 2 raspberries and a dollop of the remaining chocolate hazelnut spread.

- Frost with cream cheese frosting and top with a few more raspberries.

Cakes & Cupcakes

Tricolored Buttercream Cupcakes

Makes about 16 cupcakes

Ingredients

1	(18-oz.) pkg. white cake mix
	pink and purple food dye
1	cup unsalted butter, softened
3½	cups sifted powdered sugar
2	tsp. clear vanilla extract
2	Tbsp. water
¼	tsp. salt
	fondant flower decorations (see resources section)

Party prep: Make cupcake and buttercream up to 2 days in advance. Keep in an airtight container in the refrigerator. Allow frosting to come to room temperature before piping. Store frosted cupcake in the refrigerator up to 1 day in advance.

Styling ideas: This concept can be applied to many different color schemes. Fondant toppers can be made or bought to fit any theme that you like.

Directions:

- Preheat oven according to cake mix package directions.

- Mix cake mix according to directions.

- Divide cake batter evenly into three bowls. Color one pink, color one purple, and leave one uncolored.

- Line muffin tin with cupcake liners.

- Add a layer of pink cake batter into the bottom of each liner.

- Add another layer using the purple cake batter and repeat with the uncolored cake batter.

- Bake according to package directions and allow to cool.

- Mix butter and powdered sugar together on low speed.

- Add vanilla, water, and salt. Mix on high speed until smooth.

- Divide buttercream evenly into three bowls. Color one pink, color one purple, and leave one uncolored. Place each buttercream color in a separate piping bag.

- Pipe pink buttercream using a large round tip to create one layer of frosting. Repeat with the purple and white frostings.

- Top with fondant flower decorations.

Heart Cupcakes

Makes about 16 cupcakes

Ingredients

1   (18-oz.) pkg. strawberry cake mix

1   (18-oz.) pkg. white cake mix

1   cup unsalted butter, softened

3½ cups sifted powdered sugar

2   tsp. clear vanilla extract

2   Tbsp. water

¼   tsp. salt

confetti sprinkles

Party prep: Store frosted cupcakes in the refrigerator up to 1 day in advance.

Styling ideas: How adorable is this cupcake? You can bake other shapes into cupcakes as well using this same technique! (See p. 175 for sprinkles, liners, and cake stands.)

Directions:

- Bake strawberry cake mix according to package directions in a 9×9 pan.

- Allow to cool.

- Use a small heart-shaped cookie cutter to cut out heart-shaped mini cakes.

- Mix white cake mix according to directions and line muffin tin with cupcake liners.

- Place a tablespoon of white cake mix into the cupcake liner.

- Take one of the pink heart cakes and place it point-side down into the white cake batter so that it would be a heart if looking at it from eye level.

- Top with more cake batter to help keep it in place.

- Repeat for all the cupcakes in the muffin tin but reserve about 1 cup of cake batter.

- Bake according to package directions except set your timer for half the amount of time.

- When the timer goes off, top your cupcakes with another tablespoon of white cake batter over the heart. Cook for the remaining amount of time.

- Mix butter and powdered sugar together on low speed.

- Add vanilla, water, and salt. Mix on high speed until smooth.

- Pipe buttercream onto cooled cupcakes and top with confetti sprinkles.

Cakes & Cupcakes

Strawberry Lemon Party Skewers

Makes about 10 servings

Ingredients

1   (18-oz.) pkg. yellow cake mix

4   eggs

¾   cup vegetable oil

6   Tbsp. lemon juice, divided

1   (3.5-oz.) pkg. lemon pudding mix

2   cups powdered sugar

6   oz. strawberries

Party prep: The lemon loaf and glaze can be made up to 2 days in advance and kept in an airtight container. Slice strawberries and assemble skewers on the day of the party.

Styling ideas:: These clear party skewers (see resources section) allow the bright colors of the lemon loaf and strawberry to stand out. Add a touch of flair to the end with ribbon, washi tape, or twine.

Directions:

- Preheat oven to 350 degrees and grease a loaf pan.

- Combine the cake mix, eggs, oil, and 3 tablespoons lemon juice.

- Mix until smooth.

- Add in pudding mix and combine on low until fully incorporated.

- Immediately pour mixture into loaf pan.

- Bake for 40–50 minutes or until cooked through.

- Allow to cool before removing from loaf pan.

- In a small bowl, combine powdered sugar and the remaining lemon juice—add lemon juice to achieve desired consistency.

- Cut ½-inch slices of the lemon loaf and trim 1-inch squares.

- Slice strawberries and assemble skewers, alternating with strawberries and lemon loaf.

- Serve with the lemon glaze—allow your guests to drizzle this over their serving.

  Note: This recipe makes two lemon loaves, so there will be lots left over! Refrigerate and save for later.

Cakes & Cupcakes

Candy Cupcakes

Makes about 16 cupcakes

Ingredients

1 (18-oz.) pkg. white cake mix

1 cup unsalted butter, softened

3½ cups sifted powdered sugar

2 tsp. clear vanilla extract

2 Tbsp. water

¼ tsp. salt

 assorted candies

Party prep: Store frosted and decorated cupcakes in the refrigerator up to 1 day in advance.

Styling ideas: Using an assortment of candy, you can create flowers, hearts, and many other fun decorations! You can do this ahead of time to fit your theme or you can have your guests make them as a party activity. (See the resources section for candy vendors.)

Directions:

- Bake white cake mix according to package directions for cupcakes.

- Mix butter and powdered sugar together on low speed.

- Add vanilla, water, and salt. Mix on high speed until smooth.

- Pipe buttercream onto cooled cupcakes.

- Use assorted candy to create cute shapes.

Frozen Desserts

Chilled and delicious, these desserts will have
your guests savoring every last bite!

Three-Ingredient Ice Cream

Makes 8 servings

Ingredients

1   (14-oz.) can sweetened condensed milk

2   cups heavy cream

1   Tbsp. vanilla bean paste

Party prep: Make at least 1 day in advance and up to 1 week in advance if kept in freezer.

Styling ideas: This is a great blank slate to incorporate fun sprinkles, yummy toppings, cute ice cream containers, and creative utensils! (See the resources section.)

Directions:

- Whip sweetened condensed milk, heavy cream, and vanilla bean paste on high to form stiff peaks.

- Place mixture into a freezer-safe container and cover.

- Freeze for at least 10 hours.

Coconut Raspberry Sherbet Bars

Makes about 12 servings

Ingredients

1	(12-oz.) pkg. coconut cookies
½	quart raspberry sherbet
1	cup coconut
8	oz. whipped cream

Party prep: Can be made up to 3 days in advance. You can also precut the squares and keep them in the freezer, ready to serve, so you won't have to cut them at the party.

Styling ideas: I have served these at many girls events, and they are a big hit. They are light, full of flavor, cool, and refreshing. Since they will melt a bit, serve them on fun party plates with cute utensils.

Directions:

- Place the coconut cookies into a plastic bag and smash into a coarse crumble.

- Scoop the raspberry sherbet, coconut, and ⅔ of the crushed coconut cookie crumble into a large bowl.

- Mix gently until mostly combined.

- Fold in whipped cream.

- Spread into a 9×13 pan and top with remaining coconut cookie crumble.

- Cover and freeze for a minimum of 3 hours.

- Remove from freezer 15 minutes before serving and cut into square bars.

Frozen Desserts

Mango Strawberry Coconut Popsicles

Makes about 6 servings

Ingredients

1   recipe Mango Pineapple Smoothies (p. 96)

1   recipe Strawberry Banana Smoothies (p. 96)

1   (13-oz.) can coconut milk

5   Tbsp. powdered sugar

Party prep: These can be made up to 1 week in advance.

Styling ideas: This color combination is fun for girly parties and can be easily changed by switching up the fruit layers or dyeing the coconut layer with food dye. If you are using wooden popsicle sticks, add flair with patterned stamps, ribbon, or washi tape.

Directions:

• Make the Mango Pineapple Smoothie and pour it into the bottom third of a popsicle mold.

• Freeze for about 30 minutes.

• Make the Strawberry Banana Smoothie and pour it into the mold on top of the mango layer.

• Freeze for about 30 minutes.

• Mix the coconut milk and powdered sugar in a small bowl and pour it into the mold for the final layer.

• Freeze for a minimum of 2 hours before serving.

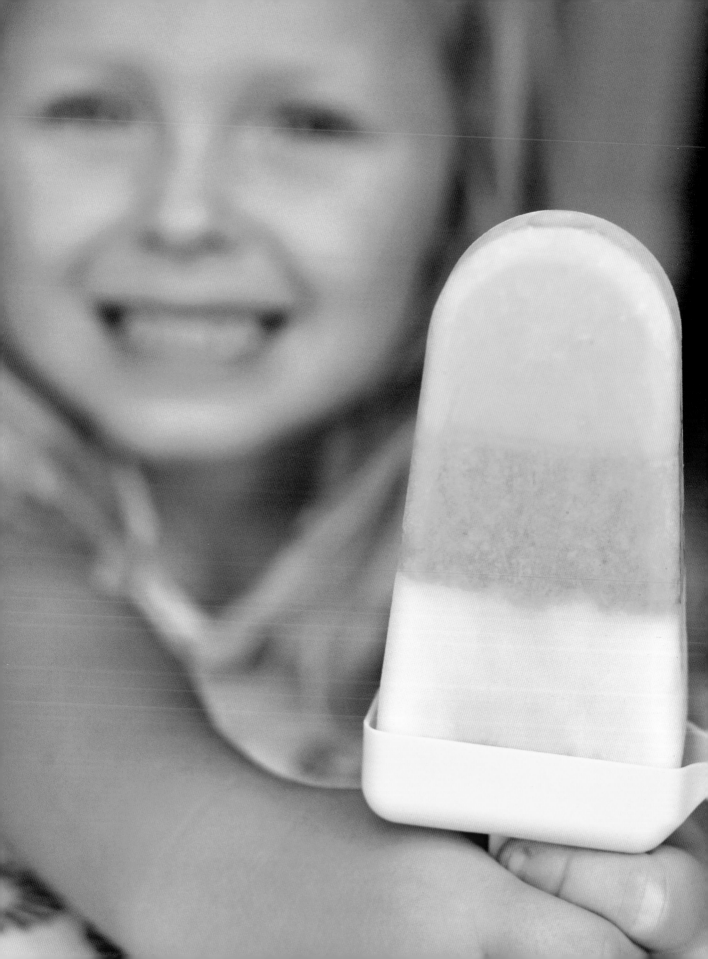

Mint Chocolate Chip Ice Cream Cupcakes

Makes about 8 servings

Ingredients

2	cups chocolate graham cracker crumbs
1	cup milk
1	pint mint chocolate chip ice cream
2	cups whipped cream topping
½	cup mini chocolate chips

Party prep: These can be made up to about 4 days in advance. You can also eliminate a step on the day of the party by freezing them with the whipped cream and chocolate chips.

Styling ideas: These can be served with the cupcake liners, giving you another opportunity to style these to your theme. They can also be styled with a party flag or printable on a toothpick in the center of the cupcake!

Directions:

- Prepare a muffin tin with cupcake liners.

- Place 2 tablespoons of chocolate graham cracker crumbs into the bottom of each cupcake liner.

- Drizzle 1 tablespoon of milk into each cupcake liner.

- Slightly defrost mint chocolate chip ice cream so it is easy to scoop and maneuver.

- Add about ¼ cup of ice cream to each liner and level off the top.

- Freeze for a minimum of 6 hours.

- When ready to serve, pipe a swirl of whipped cream and sprinkle with mini chocolate chips over the top. Serve immediately.

Frozen Desserts

Chocolate Ice Cream Bowls

Makes 12 servings

Ingredients

18   oz. chocolate chips

6   oz. frozen cherries

1   pint black cherry chocolate ice cream

Party prep: Chocolate bowls and piped designs can be made up to 3 days ahead of time and kept in the refrigerator. Thaw cherries 1 hour before serving and assemble right before serving.

Styling ideas: When creating the bowl, you can use colorful candy melts or white chocolate, or paint designs on the mold using multiple colors of chocolate! You can also pipe fun designs for the topper—hearts, stars, letters, numbers, and more!

Directions:

- Pour chocolate chips into a microwave-safe bowl.

- Microwave for 30 seconds on low power. Stir and repeat until melted and smooth.

- Pour melted chocolate into the dessert dome candy mold of your desired size (2.6-inch dome is shown in photo).

- Apply top layer of the mold and place into your refrigerator or freezer to set.

- Once hardened, remove chocolate bowls and store in the refrigerator.

- To create the swirl design, pipe some of the melted chocolate onto parchment paper and allow to set. Remove from the parchment paper and store in the refrigerator.

- An hour before serving, remove the cherries from the freezer and thaw in the refrigerator or on the counter.

- When ready to serve, remove the chocolate bowls from the refrigerator and scoop the ice cream directly into the bowl.

- Top with cherries and the piped chocolate swirl.

Sweet Treats

There is always room for more dessert!
Here are even more sweet treats for your guests to enjoy.

Raspberry Meringue Sandwiches

Makes about 24 meringues

Ingredients

4	large egg whites
1	cup sugar
1	Tbsp. meringue powder
1	tsp. raspberry extract
	pink food coloring
2	cups heavy cream
3	Tbsp. powdered sugar

Party prep: Meringues can be made and stored in an airtight container for up to 1 week. Whipped cream can be made and stored in the refrigerator 1 day in advance. Assemble sandwiches right before serving.

Styling ideas: Meringues are an awesome party treat because they are so versatile. You can pipe them into lots of shapes using different tips, and you can color them to match any party color!

Directions:

- Combine egg whites, sugar, and meringue powder in a double boiler.

- Whisk on low until sugar dissolves and liquid is foamy and hot to the touch.

- Transfer to a stand mixer with a whisk attachment.

- Whisk until stiff peaks form. Add the raspberry extract and whisk to combine.

- Add the pink food dye and whisk again to combine.

- Fill a large pastry bag with meringue and fit with a Wilton 2D tip and line baking sheets with parchment paper.

- To pipe a rose, hold the bag vertical in the center point of the rose. Begin piping and move outward in a circular movement while continuing to hold the bag vertical. Release pressure on the bag and lift the tip to finish.

- Preheat oven to 175 degrees and cook for 1½–2 hours. Leave the pans in the oven for another hour to cool.

- Whip heavy cream and powdered sugar on high until stiff peaks form.

- Take 2 meringues and sandwich them together using the whipped cream.

- Serve immediately.

Sweet Treats

Peanut Butter Chocolate Cereal Bites

Makes about 12 servings

Ingredients

2	Tbsp. butter
14	oz. marshmallows
3	Tbsp. peanut butter
3½	cups chocolate puffed rice cereal
¼	cup chocolate chips
¼	cup peanut butter chips

 Party prep: These can be made up to 2 days ahead of time. Keep in an airtight container to avoid drying out.

 Styling ideas: These would be great as a late-night sleepover snack or even for a chick flick movie night! Package them in a glassine favor bag—a great favor at any girly party.

Directions:

- Line a sheet pan with parchment paper.

- Melt butter in a large saucepan and add marshmallows on medium-low heat.

- Stir until combined and marshmallows are fully melted. Add peanut butter and stir to combine.

- Remove from heat and immediately add rice cereal, stirring to coat with marshmallows.

- Scoop out spoonfuls and place on the parchment paper.

- Let cool until you are able to handle them. Roll each spoonful into a ball.

- In a small bowl, microwave chocolate chips for 30 seconds on low power. Stir and repeat until melted and smooth.

- Drizzle melted chocolate chips over the top. Repeat the melting and drizzling with the peanut butter chips.

Sweet Treats

Ombré Marshmallows

Makes about 50 marshmallows

Ingredients

3	(.25-oz.) pkgs. unflavored gelatin
1	cup water, divided
1½	cups sugar
1	cup light corn syrup
½	tsp. salt
2	tsp. coconut extract
3	Tbsp. cornstarch
3	Tbsp. powdered sugar
	purple food dye

Party prep: This process can take some time—be sure you have enough time to do this process all the way through or the marshmallow layers will not set right. These can be made up to 2 weeks before the party.

Styling ideas: You can adapt the color to any color scheme for your party. These are also fun served on a skewer tied with a cute coordinating ribbon!

Directions:

- Place gelatin and ½ cup water in a stand mixer bowl. Set aside.

- In a small saucepan, heat remaining water, sugar, corn syrup, and salt on medium heat. Place a candy thermometer into the saucepan to monitor the temperature.

- Bring to a rolling boil and cook until candy thermometer reads 240 degrees and then remove immediately from heat.

- Using the whisk attachment on the stand mixer, turn to low speed and begin whisking water and gelatin. Slowly pour the hot syrup into the mixture as you whisk.

- Once all the syrup has been incorporated, increase your speed to high and whisk for 10 minutes.

- Add coconut extract and continue to whisk on high until the mixture is thick, is warm, and forms peaks, about 5 more minutes.

- Combine cornstarch and powdered sugar in a small bowl.

- Grease a 9×13 pan and dust with the powdered mixture. Set aside any remaining powder mixture for later.

- When marshmallow mixture is ready, remove the whisk and set aside for later.

- Scoop out one-third of the marshmallow using a greased spatula and spread onto the bottom of the pan in an even layer. The marshmallow mixture does not need to go all the way to the edge of the pan as long as it is an even layer.

- Return the bowl to the stand mixer and add a few drops of purple food dye. Whisk until the color is even throughout.

- Scoop out half of the remaining mixture on top of the first white layer in the pan. Spread evenly using a greased spatula.

- Return the bowl to the stand mixer and add a few more drops of purple food dye. Whisk until the color is even throughout.

- Scoop out the remaining mixture on top of the previous layer in the pan. Spread evenly using a greased spatula.

- Dust the top of the marshmallows (and edges if visible) with the powdered mixture. If any of the mixture remains, set aside for later.

- Rest the marshmallows, uncovered, at room temperature for 5 hours.

- Once rested, lightly dust your working surface with the powder mixture.

- Remove the marshmallows from the pan and use a pizza cutter to cut 1-inch squares of marshmallows. Dip the freshly cut marshmallows in the powder mixture to coat the sticky sides.

- Store in an airtight container for up to 2 weeks.

Sweet Treats

Cookies & Crème Truffles

Makes 12–15 servings

Ingredients

1	(18-oz.) pkg. golden Oreo cookies
8	oz. cream cheese, room temperature
12	oz. white chocolate or white candy melts
¼	cup colored sanding sugar

Party prep: These can be made up to 3 days ahead of time and kept in the refrigerator. Best served slightly chilled or at room temperature.

Styling ideas: I chose to use the golden Oreos so that you can use a light-colored chocolate or candy melt to cover it. Candy melts and sanding sugars come in a variety of fun colors and are easy to match to a specific theme.

Directions:

- Finely crush Oreo cookies.

- In a stand mixer, combine crushed Oreos with cream cheese.

- Line a sheet pan with wax paper.

- Hand-roll cookie mixture into 1-inch balls and set on the wax paper.

- Place the sheet pan in the refrigerator.

- Pour white chocolate chips or candy melts into a microwave-safe bowl.

- Microwave for 30 seconds on low power. Stir and repeat until melted and smooth.

- Remove the sheet pan from the refrigerator. Dip a truffle into the melted chocolate using a fork.

- When lifting the truffle out of the chocolate, tap the fork gently on the side of the bowl to encourage extra chocolate to run off, and scrape the back of the fork along the rim of the bowl to remove excess chocolate.

- Place the truffle back onto the lined sheet pan. While the chocolate is still wet, sprinkle sanding sugar over the top.

- Repeat with all the remaining truffles and replace back in the refrigerator to set until ready to serve.

Chocolate Parfait

Makes about 8 servings

Ingredients

1   (4-oz.) pkg. chocolate pudding mix

2   cups heavy cream

3   Tbsp. powdered sugar

2   cups graham cracker crumbs

6   oz. Kit Kats

Party prep: While the pudding can be made up to 3 days ahead of time, these should be assembled the day of the party or up to 12 hours before and kept in the refrigerator until serving.

Styling ideas: Serve these in a skinny, tall glass so that you can really see each layer. Use a star tip to pipe the whipped cream to give it added dimension.

Directions:

- Make chocolate pudding according to package directions.

- Whip heavy cream and powdered sugar together to form stiff peaks.

- Add about 2 tablespoons of graham cracker crumbs to the bottom of your serving cup. Next, layer about ¼ cup of pudding.

- Top with piped whipped cream, a sprinkle of graham cracker crumbs, and 2 Kit Kats.

Layered Fruity Gelatin Hearts

Makes about 12 (3-inch) hearts

2   (3-oz.) pkgs. orange-flavored gelatin, divided

5   (.25-oz.) pkgs. unflavored gelatin, divided

5½ cups water, divided

1½ cups coconut milk, divided

1½ cups sugar, divided

2   (3-oz.) pkgs. pineapple-flavored gelatin, divided

Party prep: This process takes some time but can be spread out over a day, adding layers as you have time. It can be made up to 4 days in advance and kept in an airtight container in the refrigerator.

Styling ideas: I love this recipe! It is super versatile for any party—change the flavor of the gelatin and change the cookie cutter shape for a whole new look!

Directions:

- In a small bowl, combine 1 package of orange-flavored gelatin, ½ package of unflavored gelatin, and 1 cup of hot water. Stir to dissolve. Allow to cool to lukewarm or room temperature.

- Pour mixture into a 9×13 pan and place it level in your refrigerator or freezer.

- Allow the gelatin to set—about 15 minutes in the freezer or 30 minutes in the refrigerator. Prepare the next layer while this sets.

- In a small saucepan, combine ½ cup water, ½ cup coconut milk, and 1 package of unflavored gelatin. Let this sit for 2 minutes.

- Add ½ cup sugar to the saucepan, turn the heat to low, and stir until dissolved.

- Remove from the heat, pour into a small bowl, and cool to lukewarm or room temperature.

- Remove the pan from the refrigerator or freezer and pour the coconut gelatin over the orange layer.

- Return the pan to the refrigerator or freezer and prepare the next layer while it sets.

- In a small bowl, combine 1 package of pineapple-flavored gelatin, ½ package of unflavored gelatin, and 1 cup hot water. Stir to dissolve. Allow to cool to lukewarm or room temperature.

- Remove the pan from the refrigerator or freezer and pour the pineapple gelatin over the coconut layer.

- Return the pan to the refrigerator or freezer.

- Repeat this process, adding more layers—coconut, orange, coconut, and then pineapple.

- When all of the layers are set, use a cookie cutter to cut out individual heart-shaped servings.

Orange Cherry Gelatin Salad

Makes about 12 servings

Ingredients

- 2 (6-oz.) pkgs. cherry-flavored gelatin
- 3 cups hot water
- 1 (16-oz.) can crushed pineapple
- 1 (12-oz.) can mandarin oranges, drained
- 6 oz. frozen cherries, thawed
- 1 recipe Whipped Cream Shapes (p. 106)

Party prep: This can be made up to 3 days ahead of time and stored airtight in the refrigerator.

Styling ideas: This recipe is a simple one, but one of the biggest hits at every party! Change up the shape of the whipped cream to add more personality to this dessert.

Directions:

- Combine cherry-flavored gelatin and hot water in a large bowl. Stir until dissolved.

- Add crushed pineapple with the juice, drained mandarin oranges, and thawed cherries.

- Stir to combine and then pour into a 9×13 pan.

- Set pan level in the refrigerator for a minimum of 4 hours.

- Cut into squares to serve and top with Whipped Cream Shapes.

Sweet Treats

Chocolate-Dipped Desserts

Makes about 12 servings

Ingredients

12 oz. chocolate chips or candy melts

assorted foods to dip

sprinkles (optional)

 Party prep: These can be made 1 day in advance and kept in a cool location in an airtight container separated with wax paper.

 Styling ideas: You have so many options for foods to dip—cookies, pretzels, marshmallows, crispy rice treats, and more. I love using skewers with a little extra punch of fun and mixing it up with different-colored candy melts! This is not only a versatile treat to serve to your guests, but it can also be a fun activity too. Have your guests dip and add decorations.

Directions:

- Pour chocolate chips or candy melts into a microwave-safe bowl.

- Microwave for 30 seconds on low power. Stir and repeat until melted and smooth.

- If using a skewer, insert that into the food item before dipping into chocolate.

- Dip each item halfway into the melted chocolate. When pulling it out, hover over the chocolate and allow the excess to drip off.

- If adding sprinkles, do so while the chocolate is wet.

- Place the dipped items on wax paper to set.

- Drizzle additional chocolate over the items while on the wax paper if desired.

S'mores Sandwich Bites

Makes about 15 servings

Ingredients

10   oz. graham crackers

6   oz. marshmallow spread

12   oz. chocolate chips

¼   cup sprinkles (optional)

Party prep: These can be made 1 day in advance and kept in a cool location in an airtight container separated with wax paper.

Styling ideas: Serve these at any rustic party—they would be perfect for a camping party, cowgirl party, or even just a girls' night!

Directions:

- Break graham crackers into bite-size pieces along the break lines.

- Prepare sandwiches by spreading marshmallow spread between 2 graham crackers.

- Pour chocolate chips into a microwave-safe bowl. Microwave for 30 seconds on low power. Stir and repeat until melted and smooth.

- Dip the cracker sandwiches halfway into the chocolate and then set them on wax paper to set. If adding sprinkles, do so while the chocolate it wet.

- Once the chocolate is set, they are ready to eat!

Candy Skewers

Makes about 10 candy skewers

Ingredients

5   oz. rainbow ribbon candy

32   oz. assorted gummy candies

3   oz. sour cherry candies

Party prep: These can be made up to 4 days in advance if kept in an airtight container.

Styling ideas: These make great party treats, and they also make great favors! To make them stand upright, add Styrofoam to a colorful container, cover with tissue paper, and stick the skewers into the Styrofoam.

Directions:

• Fold the ribbon candy back and forth a few times on top of itself and stick a thin wooden skewer through the middle.

• Slide more ribbon candy and assorted gummy candies onto the skewer in a pattern.

• Top the sharp point with a sour cherry candy.

• Repeat steps for all skewers.

Party Activities *and* Favors

One of my favorite things to do is incorporate food into the activities at the party. It allows your guests to be creative, to be innovative, and to make great memories from your event. Here are a few suggestions for incorporating some of the recipes from this book into your party:

1. Decorate Your Own Cupcake or Cookie

Bake plain cookies or cupcakes and present your guests with an array of frosting colors, sprinkles, food items, and candy to challenge their creativity! You can give them specific design challenges that go with your party theme or simply allow them to create individually. Offer prizes for the most creative or other categories to spark their interest. And, of course, they can eat their works of art or take them home as favors!

Recipes for this: Tricolored Buttercream Cupcakes (p. 128), Heart Cupcakes (p. 130), Candy Cupcakes (p. 135), Individual Fruit Pizzas (p. 109)

2. Food-Eating Contest

You may think this is just for the kids, but you would be surprised how much fun this is for adults as well! A few classic ideas you could use: donuts on a string, bobbing for apples, and pie-eating contests!

Recipes for this: Blueberry Mini Pies (p. 118)

3. Toppings Stations

I love serving food this way at events—and your guests will love it too! It is interactive and allows for individualized servings. Some ideas for types of topping bars include hot chocolate, ice cream sundaes, salads, baked potatoes, soups, vegetable cups, snack mixes, and flavored lemonades. Your guests will have fun choosing toppings and creating something that is perfect for their palate.

Recipes for this: Raspberry Mint Lemonade (p. 93), Fruity Italian Sodas (p. 100), Flavored Hot Chocolate Spoons (p. 103), Fresh Veggie Cups (p. 21), Baked Sweet Potato Skins (p. 26), Chocolate Snack Mix (p. 44), Pink Cherry Snack Mix (p. 47)

4. Fill Up a Favor Bag

Provide your guest with a do-it-yourself favor bag station. Fill jars with jelly beans, gummy worms, or any type of candy. Your guests will enjoy filling up their bags with their favorite assortments. See the resources list (p. 175) to shop for adorable favor bags and candy to match your party theme.

5. Food Olympics

Challenge your guests to myriad food activities. Although a bit messy, fishing for worms is a fun one! To play, have a pie plate full of whipped cream with a few gummy worms at the bottom—the first to get all of them wins! You could also have blindfolded taste testing, biggest bubble gum bubble contest, and popcorn toss with a partner. You can even have the girls pick team names, and award the winners with silly prizes.

Recipes for this: Cake Batter Popcorn (p. 43), Fruity Candied Popcorn (p. 40)

6. Best Cookie Contest

Break your guests up into teams and provide a basic cookie dough recipe for them. Provide extracts and mix-ins for them to create their own recipe. Bake the cookies and serve them to a designated judge in a blind taste testing!

Recipes for this: Cherry & White Chocolate Chip Cookies (p. 114), Individual Fruit Pizzas (p. 109)

7. Cake Walk

This is a simple party game, and it gives your guests something to take home as a favor. Set up a dessert table with different treats packaged individually. Tape pieces of paper on the floor in a circle with numbers on them to match the number of guests in attendance. Place coordinating numbered papers in a bowl to draw from. Play music and have your guests walk in a circle from one paper to another. When the music stops, draw a number from the hat and that person gets to go and pick a dessert from the table to take home.

Recipes for this: Any of the dessert recipes

8. Chocolate-Covered Treats

Provide your guests with an array of foods—marshmallows, pretzels, cookies, fruit, and crispy rice treats are some examples that work well. Melt chocolate and candy melts of different colors and flavors for them to dip the food into. Then they can use sprinkles or drizzle chocolate to give it added flair! Your guests can enjoy the treats at the party, or you can package them up for party favors.

Recipes for this: Chocolate-Dipped Desserts (p. 164)

9. Crafting with Food

Use candy, pasta, cereal, or other food items to create mosaic pictures, make necklaces, or decorate wooden letters that represent the guests' names, or challenge them to create a sculpture using toothpicks to connect candy together. Offer prizes for the most creative or other categories to spark their interest.

RESOURCES

Party and Baking Supplies

I shop from these adorable online party suppliers all the time. From cupcake wrappers to sprinkles to striped straws and more—they have you covered.

shoptomkat.com

karaspartyideas.com/shop

shopsweetlulu.com

sucreshop.com

bakeitpretty.com

Tools and Equipment

These are my go-to kitchen supply sites.

wilton.com

kitchenaid.com

surlatable.com

williams-sonoma.com

Decorating, Baking, Craft, and Décor Stores

While many of these stores carry baking and decorating tools and supplies, they are also great places for party decorations, cake stands, party props, and more!

Michaels

Target

Hobby Lobby

Jo-Ann

HomeGoods

Cost Plus World Market

Party City

Printable Party Designs

The printable party decorations in this book are just the tip of the iceberg for these talented designers. Be sure to check out their shops for more stunning designs.

birdsparty.com (floral fry boxes)

frogprincepaperie.com (haute chocolate collection)

Favorite Supplies

Here are some of my other favorite items for party styling.

Candy: jellybelly.com

Sparkle sticks: partiesinstyle.com

Washi tape: cutetape.com

Baker's twine: thetwinery.com

Pretty party skewers: pnpflowersinc.com

Treat pop containers: wilton.com

Party Inspiration: GetCreativeJuice.com

Be sure to stop by my site, *Creative Juice,* for more party ideas, tricks, tips, tutorials, and recipes to entertain your guest and kids with style and creativity!

Macarons

Printable templates: getcreativejuice.com/2013/08/macarons-basic-printable-template.html

Cookbook: *Gourmet French Macarons*

INDEX

Praise for *Party Food for Girls*

"*Party Food for Girls* is filled with gorgeous recipes and charming styling ideas for everything from baby showers and birthday parties to everyday get-togethers . . . all with a girly twist, of course!"

—Jennifer Sbranti, founder of *Hostess with the Mostess*

"*Party Food for Girls* is a must-have book for all hostesses! . . . Mindy's book is brimming with darling ideas, recipes, and tutorials. This book will be the new go-to for party food!"

—Courtney Whitmore, cookbook author, pizzazzerie.com

"Prepare to be inspired! Whether you want a cute afternoon treat for the little ones in your life or you are hosting a ladies' shower or lunch, *Party Food for Girls* is full of all the recipes, tips, and inspiration you'll need! From delicious appetizers to creative sweets, Mindy's book will have you ready to host the women in your life in style!"

—Glory Albin, author of *Glorious Layered Desserts*, glorioustreats.com

"If you love pretty parties and entertaining in style, this is the book for you! Filled with simple recipes, serving tips, and décor . . . everything you need to create stunning parties is at your fingertips."

—Callye Alvarado, sweetsugarbelle.com

"Mindy Cone has done it again with *Party Food for Girls*! There are so many ideas here for 'girly' entertaining. Whether it be a birthday, baby shower, bridal shower, holiday party, or girls' night out, Mindy has you covered. Her recipes are creative, fun, and beautiful to look at, and her party styling tips, like 'serve it on a stick' and 'miniaturize,' are so right on. This is definitely the modern girl's guide to entertaining . . . sweet, feminine, and oh so pretty!"

—Jillian Tohber Leslie, catchmyparty.com

About the Author

© Kristy G. Photography

Mindy Cone is an entertaining, food, and party stylist on the popular blog *Creative Juice*. She writes about everything you need to know to entertain your guests and kids with style and creativity. Her talent for perfectly themed parties combined with her love for macarons inspired her first book, *Gourmet French Macarons*. *Party Food for Girls* is her second book.

Although an East Coast girl at heart, she currently lives in Northern California with her husband and two young children.

Visit Mindy's blog at
www.getcreativejuice.com

CD with templates *included*

GOURMET FRENCH

Macarons

Unique Flavors

OVER
75

Festive Shapes

Mindy Cone

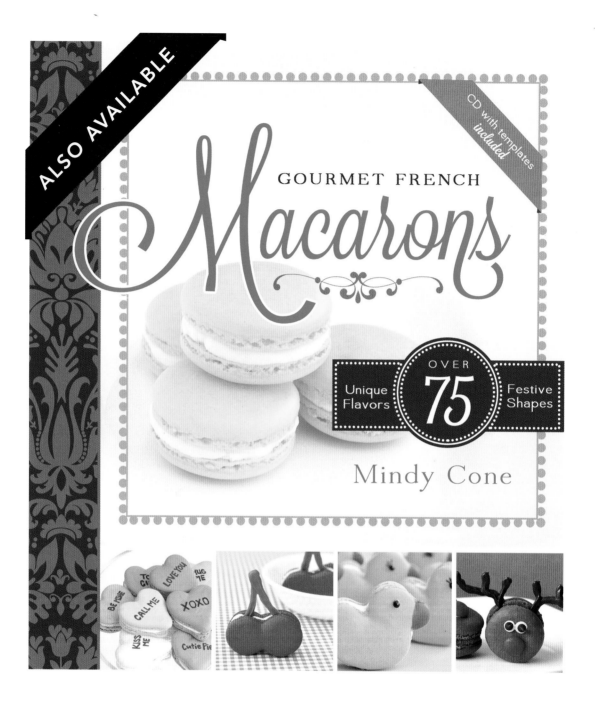